GLORIA STEINEM

GLORIA STEINEM

A Biography

Patricia Cronin Marcello

GREENWOOD BIOGRAPHIES

GREENWOOD PRESS
WESTPORT, CONNECTICUT · LONDON

Library of Congress Cataloging-in-Publication Data

Marcello, Patricia Cronin.
  Gloria Steinem : a biography / Patricia Cronin Marcello.
    p. cm. — (Greenwood biographies, ISSN 1540–4900)
  Includes bibliographical references and index.
  ISBN 0–313–32576–6 (alk. paper)
  1. Steinem, Gloria. 2. Feminists—United States—Biography. 3. Feminism—United
States. I. Title. II. Series.
HQ1413.S675M37   2004
305.42′092—dc22   2003059593
[B]

British Library Cataloguing in Publication Data is available.

Library of Congress Catalog Card Number: 2003059593
ISBN: 0–313–32576–6
ISSN: 1540–4900

First published in 2004

Greenwood Press, 88 Post Road West, Westport, CT 06881
An imprint of Greenwood Publishing Group, Inc.
www.greenwood.com

Printed in the United States of America

The paper used in this book complies with the
Permanent Paper Standard issued by the National
Information Standards Organization (Z39.48–1984).

10 9 8 7 6 5 4 3 2 1

Copyright Acknowledgments

The author and publisher gratefully acknowledge permission for use of the following materials: Interviews with Gloria Steinem, January 27, 2003 and February 2, 2003. Interviews with Carol Schmidt, February 21, 2003 and March 23, 2003.

*To the kind and generous Gloria Steinem, who allowed me her valuable time
to make this book stronger;*
*To Wendi Schnaufer, a caring editor who is not only good at her job, but also
with whom it is easy to work;*
*To my friend Carol Schmidt, who took time away from her own art to give me
her impressions of Detroit in the 1960s and the politics of emerging feminism,
which she experienced directly;*
*And to my husband, Pat, and my daughter, Shannon, without whose patience
and support, this book would not have been written.*

CONTENTS

Photo essay begins after page 75

SERIES FOREWORD

In response to high school and public library needs, Greenwood developed this distinguished series of full-length biographies specifically for student use. Prepared by field experts and professionals, these engaging biographies are tailored for high school students who need challenging yet accessible biographies. Ideal for secondary school assignments, the length, format, and subject areas are designed to meet educators' requirements and students' interests.

Greenwood offers an extensive selection of biographies spanning all curriculum related subject areas including social studies, the sciences, literature and the arts, history and politics, as well as popular culture, covering public figures and famous personalities from all time periods and backgrounds, both historic and contemporary, who have made an impact on American and/or world culture. Greenwood biographies were chosen based on comprehensive feedback from librarians and educators. Consideration was given to both curriculum relevance and inherent interest. The result is an intriguing mix of the well known and the unexpected, the saints and sinners from long-ago history and contemporary pop culture. Readers will find a wide array of subject choices from fascinating crime figures like Al Capone to inspiring pioneers like Margaret Mead, from the greatest minds of our time like Stephen Hawking to the most amazing success stories of our day like J. K. Rowling.

While the emphasis is on fact, not glorification, the books are meant to be fun to read. Each volume provides in-depth information about the subject's life from birth through childhood, the teen years, and adulthood. A thorough account relates family background and education, traces personal and professional influences, and explores struggles, accomplishments, and contributions. A timeline highlights the most significant life events against a historical perspective. Bibliographies supplement the reference value of each volume.

INTRODUCTION

Since 1934, Gloria Steinem has been evolving. The curly haired little girl, who always wore a red bathing suit so her mother could find her on a crowded Michigan beach, was forced to become responsible before her time. For eleven years, she cared for her mother, a victim of severe depression, while living in a house that should likely have been condemned.

Gloria escaped her purgatory to become an Ivy League Phi Beta Kappa, spent time living and trekking through India, and rose to become a respected writer in the New Journalism days of the early 1960s. She demonstrated for farmworkers, campaigned steadfastly for serious and atypical political candidates, dated high-profile men, and refused to ever marry.

Then, the memory of a very hard decision Gloria made in 1956 would bring an epiphany in 1969 and transform her life forever. She would become not only a feminist, who stressed equality for all and the right to reproductive freedom, but also a feminist who wanted other women to recognize that these were inalienable rights.

Gloria fully dedicated her life to spreading the word of feminism and, because of her stature and pleasing appearance, would become a media darling—through no fault of her own—bringing jealousy and vicious attacks that came from inside and outside the movement. Yet, Gloria never wanted to be a leader. She wanted to show women that they had no reason to suffer an unfulfilling life; they had a choice. Through her dedication, she and others like her transformed society. Women have come a very long way since the primal upheavals of the 1960s and 1970s, and Gloria has not stopped helping people to find self-esteem and individual freedom. She has been tireless in her efforts. From her prolific writings in high-profile magazines and for her books to the founding of Ms. magazine, she has made it evident that she has always been a champion of women's issues, even before women came to realize they had issues.

The most important element in documenting Gloria's life was her own words, via a comprehensive email interview and short telephone conversations. Other primary source documents include government documents and feminist documents, acquired online, and a personal interview with Carol Schmidt, a reporter for the *Michigan Chronicle*, an African American weekly in Detroit between 1965 and 1968. She was an officer of the local Congress of Racial Equality, while a research fellow in journalism at the University of North Carolina at Chapel Hill, and organized feminist consciousness-raising groups in the late sixties through the early 1980s. Her personal experiences during the volatile 1960s and the early days of the women's movement were invaluable in understanding the emotion and fervor of the times.

Secondary sources include scholarly works, mainstream books, periodicals, and reliable Internet sources for which the URLs are listed in the endnotes and bibliography.

TIMELINE OF EVENTS IN THE LIFE OF GLORIA STEINEM

March 25, 1934	Gloria Steinem is born in Toledo, Ohio
Fall 1944	Gloria and Ruth move to 747 Woodville Road in Toledo, Ohio
September 1948	Enters Waite High School
Summer 1951	Moves to Washington, D.C., to live with sister, Susanne
September 1951	Enters Western High School
June 12, 1952	Graduates from Western High School
September 1952	Enters Smith College, Northampton, Massachusetts
September 1954	Sails on the *Queen Mary* to Paris, and then moves on to Geneva, where she studies for her sophomore year
1956	Engaged to Blair Chotzinoff
1956	Breaks engagement and leaves to study in India; first stop London
December 1956	Realizes she is pregnant and gets an abortion
January 27, 1957	Indian visa comes through and Gloria flies to India
July 1958	Leaves Asia to return to the United States
August 1959	Supervises public relations for the World Festival of Youth and Students for Peace and Friendship in Vienna
July 1961	Receives first magazine byline
April 20, 1961	Leo Steinem dies in a car accident

1962	Named contributing editor at *Glamour* magazine
September 1962	First serious article, "The Moral Disarmament of Betty Coed," appears in *Esquire* magazine
1963	*The Beach Book* published by Viking Press
1963	"I Was a Playboy Bunny" appears in *Show* magazine and catapults Gloria to fame
January 19, 1965	Gloria's Surrealism Awards appear on *That Was the Week That Was*
April 1968	Joins the Writers and Editors War Tax Protest
April 1968	Begins writing for newly published *New York* magazine
April 1968	Raises funds for Cesar Chavez and the United Farm Workers
August 1968	Attends Democratic National Presidential Convention in Chicago, working for George McGovern
March 21, 1969	Attends abortion speak-out and becomes staunch feminist
January 1970	Begins speaking tour with Dorothy Pittman Hughes
	Testifies before Senate Subcommittee on the Equal Rights Amendment (ERA)
May 5, 1970	Speaks at Vassar College commencement ceremonies
June 1970	Attends fund-raising party for the Women's Strike Coalition at Scull estate in the Hamptons
August 9, 1970	Women's Strike for Equality
August 26, 1970	Begins group discussions of a newsletter that eventually ends up as *Ms.* magazine
January 1971	Addresses Harvard Law Review banquet
June 1971	Speaks at Smith's commencement exercises
July 9, 1971	Clay Felker agrees to finance a sample issue of *Ms.* magazine as part of *New York* magazine's year-end double issue
July 10, 1971	First meeting of the National Women's Political Caucus (NWPC)
August 16, 1971	On the cover of *Newsweek* magazine
December 20, 1971	First issue of *Ms.* magazine hits the newsstands as insert to *New York* magazine

January 1972	Works for presidential candidacies of Shirley Chisholm and George McGovern simultaneously
August 1972	Named *McCall's* Woman of the Year
December 1972	*Ms.* Foundation for Women established
February 9, 1973	First National NWPC Convention
May 9, 1975	Redstockings attack with "Redstockings Discloses Gloria Steinem's CIA Cover-Up"
December 1977	Awarded a Woodrow Wilson International Center for Scholars fellowship to write a book on feminism and politics while working at the center in Washington, D.C.
September 1978	Gives homily at St. Joan of Arc Church in Minneapolis to consternation of Catholic hierarchy
August 1979	Organized Voters for Choice
May 1980	"Feminist Notes: Linda Lovelace's Ordeal" appears in *Ms.* magazine
July 1981	Ruth Steinem dies
November 1982	Chosen as one of the most influential women in America by *New York Times* magazine
1983	Second book, *Outrageous Acts and Everyday Rebellions,* published
January 1984	Appears on Mr. Blackwell's Worst Dressed List
March 25, 1984	Fiftieth birthday party held at the Waldorf Astoria
February 25, 1985	TV movie version of "A Bunny's Tale" is broadcast with Kirstie Alley as Gloria
November 1985	Begins her battle with breast cancer
1986	*Marilyn: Norma Jeane* first published
May 1986	Begins psychotherapy
May 1986	Appears with interview segments on the *Today Show*
November 1987	*Ms.* magazine sold to Fairfax Publications (U.S.) Ltd.
1988	Hired by Random House as contributing editor
October 1989	*Ms.* sold to Dale Lang of Lang Communications, Inc.
August 1990	*Ms.* reborn as bimonthly with no advertising and Robin Morgan as editor

January 1992	*Revolution from Within* is published
Fall 1993	Inducted into the Women's Hall of Fame
January 1994	*Moving Beyond Words* is published
March 25, 1994	Surprise sixtieth birthday party held for Gloria at Jezebel's restaurant in New York
June 1995	Goes on safari to the Kalahari Desert in Botswana
May 1997	*Ms.* sold to Jay MacDonald
December 1998	Liberty Media Foundation buys back *Ms.*
September 3, 2000	Marries David Bale
2001	Gloria Steinem Leadership Institute founded
December 31, 2001	Feminist Majority Foundation assumes ownership of *Ms.*
February 13, 2002	Speaks at the Commonwealth Club of California
March 2002	*Ms.* celebrates its thirtieth anniversary, with Gloria on the cover
June 2003	Wins the American Association of University Women's Educational Foundation's award for achievement
March 4, 2003	Speaks at Indiana University East Women's Commission Conference

Chapter 1

A BACKGROUND FOR LEADERSHIP

Long before scientists mapped the genome, it seemed obvious that certain family qualities carried through generations. The Roosevelts and Kennedys may have political genes; the Wyeths, genes of artistry; and the Barrymores, genes for acting. This hereditary phenomenon also seems true of Gloria Steinem. Her family included writers, and even one of them was a feminist. To no surprise, Gloria developed as a prolific journalist and the foremost champion of women's rights.

Her maternal grandmother, Marie (who Gloria and her sister would later call O'Momie), was born in Dunkirk, Ohio, in 1871, the second of six children. She attended teacher's college and taught school for a short time before working in the Recorder of Deeds office in Dunkirk. She lived in a boarding house, owned by Gloria's great grandparents, Johannes and Louise Ochs (pronounced Oaks).

While in her late teens, Marie and a boarder named Joseph Nuneviller fell in love; however, they were forced to keep their relationship secret. During the late Victorian era, a time of strict morals, such unions—between a boarder and the boarding house owner's daughter—were thought to be improper, and so this situation was treated as a family secret.

Nuneviller was a second-generation American, born in Portsmouth, New Hampshire, in 1867. Family history recalls that his father arrived in the New World from Germany, lashed to the mast of a ship, a survivor of a terrible storm off the coast of New Jersey. Nuneviller was a quiet man, a railroad engineer, who always ate his dessert first in case he was abruptly called to duty. He wore a suit jacket over his engineer's overalls and a bowler hat atop his head, no doubt, at his wife's insistence, as it made him appear more sophisticated.

Sedate, working-class Nuneviller was not the ideal husband for Marie Ochs, who had changed her name from Mary Catherine to Marie, perhaps because the name Marie seemed more genteel. She always aspired to a middle-class life—if not for herself, then certainly for her two daughters.

Ruth, who would become Gloria's mother, and Emma Janette, called Janey by the family, were born in 1898 and 1900 respectively. Marie pressed the girls to do well in school and used the family's complimentary railroad pass to travel to New York City, where they would explore hotels and peek through windows of elegant shops. Via these expeditions, Marie hoped to expose her daughters to the life she aimed for them to pursue. Yet, her actions had an opposite effect on Ruth, whose resultant feelings of deprivation would stay with her throughout her years.

MARIE PRIMES HER GIRLS FOR LIFE

Marie's ambitions for her daughters had her making clothes for them to save money and she made extra cash by writing sermons for a Scotch Presbyterian minister in the church next door. Gloria would later remark, "Her working-class husband needed the money she earned, and she wished that he could keep her in leisure, that she didn't have to do such physical chores."[1] Nevertheless, Marie persisted, knowing that she had reached her level in life but would not abide it for her daughters. Marie was determined to instill independence in her girls, so that they could achieve what she had been unable to attain.

In this pursuit, Marie often behaved insensitively toward Ruth and Janey, in order to teach them restraint. When Ruth was an infant, Marie abruptly decided to stop breastfeeding and handed the baby over to a family friend, until she was weaned. Only a short time later, she found Ruth exploring her genitals, as toddlers are bound to do when they come out of diapers. Yet, instead of trying to distract Ruth from the behavior with toys or other activities, she provided clear negative reinforcement by slapping Ruth so hard that she reeled across the kitchen linoleum. Marie often left both girls alone, as well, without a mention of where she was going or when she would return, to provide them with some self-reliance. However, her behavior instilled a lifelong terror of being alone in Ruth. She also carried feelings of inadequacy, as sister Janey seemed more willing to adapt to their mother's wishes, thus garnering more maternal attention.

Marie also counseled the girls not to marry. She planned that they attend a teachers' college, as she had. Even in the beginning of the twenti-

eth century, when work-ethical Americans were just beginning to popu-
larize the concept of the weekend, it was unusual for girls to seek higher
education. As a rule, regardless of their potential, women were restricted
to pink collar jobs, such as secretary, nurse, librarian, and other positions
considered feminine in nature. In the Nuneviller family, it was fixed that
both girls would attend college and become teachers. Marie considered
teaching to be the only acceptable profession for women and saw a life
free of marriage and children as one of self-preservation and satisfaction.

Ruth started at Oberlin College, a private school in Ohio, in 1916,
while Janey went directly to the University of Wisconsin, a more-
affordable state school, as the money for private schooling had run out.
At Oberlin, Ruth majored in math and earned the nickname Billy from
her friends but, in her junior year, was forced to transfer to the University
of Toledo—also a state supported school—due to financial hardship. She
lived at home, and to supplement the family's earnings, Ruth also held a
job as a part-time bookkeeper in an elegant lingerie shop.

Living at home again, Ruth had to endure the incessant lectures on the
benefits of a teacher's life from her mother but Ruth's dream was not to be
a teacher. At the first opportunity, she planned to run away to New York
to become a newspaper journalist. Janey, of course, would listen to her
mother and become a high school teacher in Toledo.

Gloria remembers her grandmother as kind and as the person who
taught her to play solitaire.

> [She] made me small cream pies out of the extra dough when
> she baked. I have an impression that she was hard working,
> ambitious and...difficult to have as a mother—though this is
> the side I heard from my own mother. Sometime during my
> teens, she succumbed to a form of dementia and was bedridden
> and cared for by my Aunt Janey for years. My other lasting
> sense memories are the smell of lavender on her handkerchief,
> her strong will, and her love for listening to—and betting on—
> baseball games on the radio.[2]

GLORIA'S JEWISH GRANDMOTHER

Just as Marie Nuneviller's influence would later affect the life of her
granddaughter, Gloria's paternal grandmother Pauline Steinem would
also make a significant impact. Yet, Pauline died when Gloria was five
years old. Gloria did not consider her grandmother's accomplishments
particularly significant for her own life, until much later.

Gloria's grandfather, Joseph Steinem, prospered in real estate in Toledo, Ohio, and achieved the type of middle-class existence for his family that Marie Nuneviller so strongly desired. A German Jew, he immigrated to America before meeting Gloria's grandmother and acquired a few inexpensive rental properties and a small brewery. When he had enough money, at age 33, he went back to Germany to choose a wife.

Although first interested in the older daughter of a German cantor (a Jewish singer who leads the musical part of a religious service) by the name of Perlmutter, he fell instantly in love with her younger sister, Pauline, and asked for her hand instead. The engagement was set on two stipulations: that Joseph return 21-year-old Pauline to Germany for frequent visits and that he close his brewery. Not only was Pauline a strict vegetarian but she was also vehemently opposed to alcoholic beverages to the extent that she used paste vanilla in her cooking rather than use an extract that contained alcohol. However, wine was an acceptable libation for others.

Joseph agreed to both conditions and the couple was married in 1884. They remained in Munich until 1887, where they had their first son Edgar, and then came back to the United States to settle in Toledo. The Steinems would come to have three more sons—Jesse, Clarence, and Leo, Gloria's father.

While Joseph was successful in business, Pauline Steinem became the more influential of the two. At a time when women were sometimes told that higher education was dangerous to their reproductive systems, she had graduated from the Teacher's Seminary at Memmington, Bavaria, and was also educated in traditional arts, such as fine embroidery. Pauline attained U.S. citizenship, learned to speak English without a trace of a German accent, and ultimately became an ardent suffragette. She was the first woman on the Toledo Board of Education and the city's first female elected official. A great organizer of women's groups, Pauline even addressed the U.S. Congress on women's right to vote. As one of two American delegates, she attended the International Council on Women, held in Switzerland in 1908, and was so active nationally on education and women's suffrage that she was listed in *Who's Who in America* between 1910 and 1925.

A reformed Jew, who believed in the right of an individual to subscribe to selected beliefs or practices, Pauline was also involved in the Hebrew Ladies' Benevolent Society, a group that helped the community's poor, regardless of religion. And she was the president of the Jewish Free Loan Association of Toledo, which made interest free loans to help women pay for rent, medical bills, education, and other personal requirements, while men applied mainly to start business ventures. Pauline was also involved in the founding of Macomber Vocational High School, the first public school for vocational education in Toledo.

PUBLIC FEMINIST, PRIVATE JEWISH MOTHER

Though Pauline stressed women's equality in suffrage, she was not equal at home. She kept an immaculate house and, disregarding her own vegetarianism and teetotalism, Pauline fed her sons and husband meat and wine and saw to their every comfort. Gloria remarked, "Perhaps like many suffragists, my grandmother was a public feminist and a private isolationist."[3]

Pauline was also drawn to the study of Theosophy because of her beliefs in social justice and the moral life. This religious philosophy is based on mystical insight into the nature of God and includes beliefs from other Eastern religions, such as Buddhism and Brahmanism, especially in those religions' attitudes toward reincarnation and spiritual growth. Pauline became a leading member of the Theosophical Society in Toledo and once wrote in the Toledo *Blade,* the leading newspaper of Toledo, that Theosophy concentrated on the brotherhood of man, without discrimination. Ruth was closer to her mother-in-law than her own mother and also became interested in Theosophy. She would later pass Theosophist ideals on to her own children.

As generous with her money as she was with her time and ideas, Pauline retired from public life after 1921 and lived comfortably with Joseph. He died suddenly in 1929, after a six-day illness that was probably pneumonia, although it was never formally diagnosed. The Steinem family blames his death on the stock market crash earlier that year, which made him worry over family finances so much that he trudged through the snow every day to check on his declining investments. They say he died of a broken heart due to the loss of personal wealth, which he had worked so hard throughout his life to attain.

Nonetheless, he left a substantial estate. Pauline used much of the money willed to her and her $500 a month income, worth nearly 10 times that much today, to ransom German Jews from Nazi Germany and send them to Israel. Although the family thought she was spending too much on this effort, Pauline's generosity and compassion for others would be echoed in her granddaughter's life in years to come.

TWO WITS UNITE

Pauline's fourth and youngest son, Leo, was not quite as steadfast as his mother was, though he was a bit of an organizer as well. People enjoyed his quick wit and intelligence, and while attending the University of Toledo, he organized parties and dances. In 1919, he began a student newspaper—the *Universi-Teaser*—funded by his own and his friend Samuel Steinback's money, and they peddled the paper throughout the campus for five cents a copy. During the first weeks of the *Universi-Teaser's* publication, Leo hired Ruth Nuneviller because of his attraction to the auburn-haired girl and when he learned of her writing talents, he made her the paper's first literary editor. By the fall of 1920, they had attained backing from the university and became the campus rag, renamed simply, *The Teaser*.

Through the newspaper, Ruth published some of her own stories, one of which was a mystery entitled "The Tragedy Among the Waterpipes," and by the fall of 1919, she became the paper's editor in chief. In 1920, she took on writing the humor column, "Answers by Miss Anne Circe," which had previously been written by Leo.

Although Leo still wrote for the paper, he organized even more groups, such as the literary society, for which he was unanimously elected president. As the product of liberal parents who always lectured after his failures but handed him money to assuage any dilemma, Leo was spoiled and self-indulgent and, though he had great ambitions and always wanted to make it big, he lacked one important quality—drive. In that respect, he and Ruth differed, as Marie had instilled a strong work ethic in her.

He and Ruth seemed to share similar senses of humor, however, which drew them together. But while Ruth was an exceptional student with a talent for mathematics and poetry, Leo, although intelligent, was not intellectual and never finished his education. He went through life waiting to make the big, easy score, without ever considering that it would come through a diligent career and he was fatally attracted to show business. Gloria would one day quip, "My father had two points of pride. He never wore a hat and never had a job."[4]

But he was not the only son of his wealthy family to have adjustment problems. Gloria's uncle Ed threw away a brilliant career as an electrical engineer to become the town handyman. He went from being touted as Best Dressed to a slovenly appearance, left his educated wife to marry another less gifted woman, and lived in a house with walls patched with metal signs to stop the wind. Yet, he never discussed his complete metamorphosis and was highly competent at his work. He never asked for help from anyone and charged only for the materials he used, plus 10 percent for his labor.

REBELLIOUS ROOTS

Defiance of normal society appeared on both sides of Gloria's family. While her mother's early rebellions were not as marked as those of her uncle, at a time when girls wore only dresses, Ruth would boldly don her father's overalls to work in the garden. Though her Scotch Presbyterian church looked upon dancing as evil, Ruth ignored the conviction and found the courage to attend dances regularly, proving that both of Gloria's parents were undisciplined in one way or another.

On a date in the summer of 1921, after knowing each other for two years, Leo suddenly stopped the car and asked Ruth to be his wife. Without much hesitation, Ruth agreed and they found a justice of the peace to marry them that day. But Ruth's anxiety over her mother finding out made her plead with Leo to keep the marriage secret. So, they returned to their parents' homes and announced that they had become engaged.

Leo's family was not pleased about the union, since Ruth was not Jewish, but even religious chauvinism could not keep the couple apart, and a few months later they were married in a formal ceremony at Ruth's home. Still, members from each family boycotted their mixed marriage between the Jew and the Christian, although Pauline welcomed Ruth to the family and they became very close.[5] Leo and Ruth would keep their first marriage a secret from the family, until Janey found the original marriage certificate years later and they were forced to admit their union.

After the wedding, Leo's parents were generous enough to provide the newlyweds a plot of land in Toledo and the funds to build a house. Ruth had promised her mother to try teaching for a year and then, if she did not like it, to get a job with a newspaper. Although it probably led to some bitterness between mother and daughter, Ruth quit teaching calculus to work for the *News Bee*, another Toledo daily, which soon after was bought by the Toledo *Blade*. Because a woman's byline was unacceptable at the time, she published her articles under the name Duncan Mackenzie. At the *Blade*, she became responsible for two pages of news for each edition.

Leo worked at several jobs, including taking photographs for ad agencies. As opposed to Ruth's indoctrination of social climbing, which always had her anxious about debt, Leo took a more casual attitude about money and worked much less seriously.

MR. SHOWBIZ RAISES A FAMILY

Leo and Ruth's first daughter, Susanne, was born in 1925, and Ruth took a year away from work to raise her. They rented a cottage about 54 miles outside Toledo that summer, at Clark Lake, Michigan. While vacationing, Leo had a brainstorm. Seeing very few cottages around the lake, he decided it would be a good place for an entrepreneur, like himself, to build a resort and so, with the help of his father, he bought 30 acres around the lake. Leo had sand added to the banks of the lake and called his resort Ocean Beach. The following year, he had a Mediterranean-style family home built on the site, large enough to accommodate the many guests who would come to visit.

Two years later, Leo had a dance pavilion built at the end of a 100-foot pier so that guests could enjoy dancing, under the stars and over the water, to Big Band sounds. While Ocean Beach was at its peak, famous band-leaders, such as Harry James, Guy Lombardo, and musician and composer Duke Ellington, made the resort a stop on their Midwest tours. The only drawback was Clark Lake's isolation. Those wishing to visit the retreat would be virtually stranded in the woods, and it was not a good place to spend cold winters without heat.

During the first few winters, the family retreated to Toledo, where in 1926, Ruth returned to work at the Toledo *Blade*; both grandmothers, Marie and Pauline, although mostly Pauline, helped watch the baby, Susanne. Ruth was about to be christened the Sunday editor, making her the highest paid employee, male or female, on the *Blade* staff. Leo increased his real estate holdings: including more Clark Lake property, eight thousand acres of pine forest, a filling station in Georgia, and a pecan orchard in Florida. And in its first summer, Ocean Beach grossed $50,000, which would be roughly worth $500,000 today. Ruth bought her clothes at the finest shops in Toledo, and Susanne went to a private school.

But Marie continued to torment Ruth, complaining that Leo was an inadequate husband. Her admonitions rose as, in the summer of 1929, Leo added a wooden toboggan run next to the pier at Ocean Beach in order for swimmers to slide into the water, and a 17-year-old boy was killed due to his own negligence in securing a safety feature of the ride. Ruth witnessed the accident and was so upset that her doctor, Kenneth Howard, a fraternity brother of Leo's, gave her sedation in the form of chloral hydrate and potassium bromide, commonly known as knockout drops in larger quantities. Trusting her friend and physician, Ruth saw the medication as an effective way to relieve her anxiety. No one knew how important the remedy would become to Ruth's life.

TERRIBLE OCCURRENCES LEAD TO A SPECIAL WISH

Near the end of that year, Ruth's tensions mounted. In October, the stock market crashed, and Leo's father died in December. Upsetting though those events were, they were only a precursor to another bad year. In February 1930, Ruth's own father died, and she became progressively more reliant on Doc Howard's medicine. Also in that year, Ruth had a miscarriage—a son the couple named Tom—which left Ruth infirm for a long while. Marie had insisted upon calling her chiropractor to attend the birth, rather than Doctor Howard, and Ruth nearly bled to death. Then, at 32, Ruth had her first nervous breakdown. She persistently clung to Leo and went days without sleep. Eventually, she stayed in a Toledo sanatorium for several months.

Leo was Susanne's sole caregiver while her mother was hospitalized and spoiled her with calorie-laden foods. Gloria later said, "I think that my sister feels that living with him, by herself, all alone, while my mother was in the mental hospital, was the beginning of her weight problem, and she resents that."[6] Leo, though thin in his college years, would come to weigh 300 pounds. Susanne would fight a weight problem throughout her life, and Gloria would become such a phobic about gaining weight that she often neglected to eat.

When Ruth came home from the hospital, she had learned to hide her emotional problems. Susanne saw a mother who was both capable and witty, and the world seemed better to her, until the family moved permanently to Clark Lake, which did nothing to please or help Ruth's mental state. She would never again work as a journalist, and the move meant giving up friends and family. To make matters worse, winters would be terribly lonely, as most residents only lived near the resort during summer months. Still, as moving would help them to economize, Ruth agreed. They sold the Toledo house, and Ruth continued to rely on Doc Howard's medicine.

When Susanne was about eight years old, she mentioned that she would like to have a little sister. She needed help taking care of all the animals they had given her—a lamb, a collie, bunnies, and chicks—as well as her two dolls, Anne and Gloria. Ruth told Sue to pray for a sibling, and late in 1933, she got her wish. Ruth was pregnant.

Bravely foregoing her Doc Howard's throughout her pregnancy, Ruth delivered another daughter on March 25, 1934. Because Sue had waited so patiently, her parents even allowed her to name the baby, and she did—after her doll Gloria. Although Ruth and Leo had planned to name the baby Cynthia, Gloria worked well with the added middle name of Marie in honor of Ruth's mother. That day, a leader, who would help to change the world, was born. Interestingly enough, her birth announcement read World Premiere Appearance. Ruth and Leo had no way of knowing how appropriate that statement would be.

LIFE WITH RUTH AND LEO

In 1934, Franklin D. Roosevelt was President of the United States and the Great Depression was underway with an unemployment rate of 22 percent. Along with the birth of Gloria Steinem, other notable global events took shape. In Europe, the world lost its premiere female scientist—Marie Curie, who died on July 4 from radiation poisoning in a sanatorium in France. A one-man crime wave was halted when bank robber John Dillinger was shot and killed by FBI special agents on July 22, as he reached for his gun outside the Biograph Theater in Chicago, Illinois. Ninety-five percent of registered voters made Adolf Hitler Führer of Germany on August 19, giving him absolute power over that country and its citizens. In India, pacifist leader Mohandas Gandhi announced his decision to retire from politics on September 17. And in that same month, the *Queen Mary* was launched by Her Majesty Queen Mary, wife of King George V of England.

Neoclassic novels, such as F. Scott Fitzgerald's *Tender Is the Night,* Henry Miller's *The Tropic of Cancer,* and James Hilton's *Good-Bye Mr. Chips,* were published in 1934. At the movies were *The Thin Man,* with William Powell and Myrna Loy as Nick and Nora Charles, and *It Happened One Night,* which won five Academy Awards that year: best picture, best actor (Clark Gable), best actress (Claudette Colbert), best director (Frank Capra), and best adaptation (Robert Riskin). Cole Porter sang "Anything Goes." In addition to Gloria Steinem and consumer advocate Ralph Nader being born in America, Sophia Loren was born in Italy, and in Canada, the Dionne Quintuplets were born, the first quintuple births to survive infancy. Not even the Depression could suppress the human drive to procreate. Life, although less than comfortable for the masses, went on.

For the first 10 years of her life, Gloria was loved and pampered, as any adorable child might be. The Steinem family lived in the Mediterranean-style, three bedroom house on Clark Lake. Ruth painted silver stars on the sky-blue ceiling of Gloria's room, tulips on the walls down at the green baseboards, and made it a beautiful garden of little-girl dreams.

Outside, little pudgy-cheeked, dark-haired Gloria, who people often compared to Shirley Temple, ran wild, looking for lost change that often slid between the cracks in the floorboards of the pier, capturing small aquatic creatures and letting them go, living in her bathing suit, and falling asleep to Big Band sounds. Her swimsuit was always red so that her mother could spot her among the crowd, and about once a month her big sister Susanne tackled her with a comb to detangle her untended hair. Gloria also recalled:

I waded in the lake under the pier to look for coins that customers at the summer resort might have dropped through the cracks. I also stayed up all night to read—once I escaped into a story, I just kept going to the end. Sometimes, my father would come home at 3 A.M. and wake me so he would have a companion for a late night swim. I loved that. I also drove my sister crazy by being the nine-years-younger sister who wanted to follow her around everywhere.[7]

Gloria got much of what she wanted, regardless of the cost. Piano lessons, puppies, and even her own horse with a Western saddle were not out of the question. But she found a new passion when a local farmer's wife came to help Ruth cook for the performing band members, and her daughter, Jackie, became Gloria's best friend.

They found a common interest in tap dancing, although Gloria was the driving force. She said, "At the Pier, there was a cigarette girl—a young woman who sold cigarettes and sundries from a tray she carried table to table—who taught me to tap dance."[8] She and Jackie then took tap dancing lessons in Jackson, the nearest town. Between the time she started dancing until about age nine, Gloria danced everywhere she went, often to the dismay of her parents, who often claimed, in jest, not to know her.

AN UNUSUAL LIFESTYLE

By about age nine, however, Gloria became conscious of herself and of her family's unusual lifestyle. Since Gloria had been about four years old, Susanne lived in the Jackson YWCA during the week, in order to attend regular high school classes in preparation for college. So, Gloria was left alone with her father, who, although handsome, was obese and sometimes sloppy. He avoided alcohol and cigarettes but he loved food. Her mother had become depressed and manic—at times, lucent and even witty, while at other times, morose and suspicious. Gloria, recognizing that they were not a typical family, began to feel somewhat insecure about her life.

The Steinems' home lacked basic amenities. There was no central heat, as the house had been built for use only in the summer. Leo claimed that he had neglected to put in a furnace for a reason: If the house was too warm, Ruth would never agree to leave it in the winter, and they always traveled to Florida or California in the coldest months. Leo fashioned himself as a traveling antiques dealer and would buy and sell goods along the way to their winter stops. The house did have a fireplace and a wood stove, and, although these provided some warmth, they were inadequate for heating the entire house. Rather than chopping logs, Leo's indolent method of fueling the fire was to shove a whole log into the fireplace and, as it burned down, to kick it further into the fire. The house had no bath or shower, either. To wash, the family took bars of soap into the lake with them, which was impossible in the depths of winter.

Even without conveniences, the Steinems had happy times, too. Leo read the Sunday comics to Gloria before she could read them herself, and they made long wish lists for Christmas—one might call them fantasy wish lists: Gloria's included a ranch with Palomino horses, Susanne's listed jewel-encrusted opera glasses, Leo's had $50,000, and Ruth's included knowing her next incarnation. The girls were also allowed to have parties now and then, including an ice-skating party for Gloria on the lake and a Halloween party for Susanne complete with a haunted house tour. And there was always the pier, with some type of activity going on, which helped Gloria to forget that the Steinem's did not live like other people—not that their lifestyle was bad. It suited their needs and broadened the girls' horizons but it was not what most kids would think of as normal. Gloria came to realize that not all families were alike and, as an adult, once wrote, "The idea that there is only one family form is really pure [bull]."[9]

However, the world perceived the nine-to-five father and the stay-at-home mother, living in one house together with the children attending formal school as the norm. Throughout these times, Ruth was never comfortable. Leo was constantly increasing the family debt without telling her, and she worried constantly about money. Gloria remembers bill collectors calling and coming to the door. And Gloria was often the one that answered these calls, as the collectors were not apt to discuss matters with a child. Leo even went to great lengths to avoid trouble. He parked the car far from their property at times so that it would not be repossessed.

Dodging bill collectors was a game for Leo, but for Ruth, his shenanigans were pure horror. She never knew when the house of cards he had built would come crashing down around them. Gloria once remarked of her parents, "My father was the financially irresponsible member of the family, always getting into debt. He taught me to live with insecurity, which is why I could become a writer and a feminist organizer, and [my mother] taught me to remember that disaster could strike."[10]

Ruth could be a good mother in her lucid moments, and the children were never hit or humiliated. Gloria said,

My mother's first main rule was to tell the truth. If she thought either my sister or I was fibbing, she'd say, 'Truly, truly.' Then we had to respond with the real truth. The second rule was never to let the sun set on our anger. My father treated me like a companion, a playmate, and an equal—whether it was taking me with him to movies I was too little to understand, or asking me to help him with his antique selling.[11]

Ruth also gave her girls the gift of self-esteem. "Over and over again, in every way she knew how, she told us that we didn't need to earn her love. We were loved and valued (and therefore we were lovable and valuable) exactly as we were."[12] Ruth told her daughters that she did not own them but, as their mother, was only there to help them to become themselves.

NOTES

1. Steinem, *Moving Beyond Words*, p. 121.

2. Gloria Steinem, interview with author, 27 January 2003.

3. Steinem, *Outrageous Acts*, p. 163 (reprint ed.).

4. Quoted in Marcia Cohen, *The Sisterhood. The True Story of the Women Who Changed the World* (New York: Simon and Schuster, 1988), p. 41.

5. In later years, Ruth would become closer to Pauline than she was to her own mother. Yet, Gloria did not feel this was necessarily a good relationship. Ruth, who suffered from an insufferable insecurity complex, saw Pauline as a superwoman who could not only succeed in the world, but also be a superb Jewish mother to her sons, and Ruth's worship of her mother-in-law only made her feelings of self-worth decrease.

6. Quoted in Carolyn G. Heilbrun, *The Education of a Woman* (New York: Dial Press, 1995), p. 15.

7. Steinem, interview, 27 January 2003.

8. Ibid.

9. Gloria Steinem, "Address to Feminist Family Values Forum," *feminist.com*, May 1996, http://www.feminist.com/resources/artspeech/family/ffvfsteinem.htm.

10. Gutner, "A Feminist Icon," pp. 116–18.

11. Steinem, interview, 27 January 2003.

12. Steinem, *Revolution from Within*, p. 65.

Chapter 2

LIFE ON THE ROAD AND IN TOLEDO

When Gloria was around six years old, Ruth had become so dependent on the medicine that Dr. Howard had given her following the tragedy at Ocean Beach that Leo assumed the chores of marketing and cooking. Gloria remembered, "We would bring home all kinds of foods—cold cuts and bread, and sandwich spread, and ice cream—and would just make food when we wanted it."[1] She does not remember ever sitting down at a family dinner table. Her dad mainly heated food from cans. Franco-American brand spaghetti was one of her favorites.

Since Ocean Beach was a seasonal business, Leo moved the family to warmer climates during winter months, pulling a standard-size trailer along behind their car. Consequently, the girls never attended a formal school full-time and their departure was sometimes quite sudden to the extent that a sink full of dirty dishes would be left behind, awaiting their return in the spring, and the family packed so quickly that basic items needed for the winter were often left behind.

The girls were mainly bored riding in the car during these trips, as are most children. Gloria once attributed learning to read to candy wrappers and ubiquitous Burma Shave signs along the highway. The billboards usually had several parts, with one line of each jingle per sign, placed at intervals along the road. The last sign always read "Burma-Shave." The signs had verses, like this: "To kiss a mug...that's like a cactus...takes more nerve...than it does practice...Burma-Shave."[2]

Toward evening, Leo would look for a trailer park, where the family could take showers. In lieu of a park, they stayed in motels but preferred the economy of living in the trailer; however, once they reached their destination, they lived in the trailer full-time. In Florida, they parked at

Clearwater Beach and, in California, at Laguna Beach. Although both places are now heavily populated, the spots were relatively deserted at that time.

While parked in Florida or California during World War II, the family had to follow the rules of Civil Defense and use blackout curtains on the windows of their trailer, so as not to emit light for fear that the enemy might use the light to spot targets on land. Even in outside darkness, they were not permitted to use flashlights, and Gloria found this to be quite an adventure.

Just after Pearl Harbor in 1942, German submarines had opened Operation Drumbeat. The plan was to use light from coastal cities to silhouette American tankers in East Coast shipping lanes and to sink them, as the lanes were virtually undefended. The Germans ruined nearly 400 ships and killed thousands of Americans during the operation, and dozens of these ships had been torpedoed just off the east and west coasts of Florida.

Rumors spread about German sailors leaving U-boats and coming ashore. Supposedly, a group showed up in a nearby bar, held the barman at gunpoint while drinking some beers, and then headed back out to sea. These stories filled Gloria's imagination and made the Florida trip that year one to remember. As she matured, her insecurities seemed to fade. "I fell in love with instability," she remembered. "I always thought that the worst thing would be to know what was going to happen next year. Because if you didn't know, it could be wonderful!"[3] Her dad was always coming up with new inventions and plans to make a million. Who knew what the future held in store?

Gloria spent some of her own time in show business, tap dancing for local clubs and performing in civic productions in Michigan. She wanted to be a dancer and earned small fees for her performances, which encouraged her even further.

UNCONVENTIONAL EDUCATION

Because the family always headed off for warmer sites around Christmas or Thanksgiving, Gloria had only partial years of formal schooling. When they returned to Michigan, she usually did not finish the school year because they left for their winter travels in autumn. Some years Gloria did not go to school at all. This erratic education caused her to have huge holes in her basic knowledge. Although she spent a great deal of time with adults and had a broad vocabulary, she did not know her multiplication tables and could not spell very well. Her participation in normal schoolyard games, such as jump rope, tag, or jacks, was spotty throughout her childhood years. However, when she penned an insightful, well-written poem for Thanksgiving during the short time she attended second grade, her teacher would not believe that she wrote it herself because it was so professional.

Gloria had learned to read by age four and was a voracious reader. Leo fashioned himself as a traveling antiques dealer and would buy and sell goods along the way to their winter stops. He often bought whole book collections just to get first editions, which always sold at a good price. From the remaining books, Gloria found a myriad of interesting material to keep satisfied.

> My favorite subjects were any in which there were stories, reading, and narrative. I read the oddest things: a series of novels about a family in *The White Oaks of Jalna*, another one about a shipping line, books about civil war battles, and quite a racy novel I didn't understand called *Silk Straps*. But my favorites included all of Louisa May Alcott—all her adult novels and short stories as well as the young people's books—plus books on horses, *Spurs for Antonia*, and all of C. W. Anderson. I love the *Encyclopedia Britannica's* many volumes of fairy tales and the poems of Edna St. Vincent Millay (my mother's favorite).[4]

Gloria also read every book in the Nancy Drew series that she could find as well as the Hardy Boys volumes, although she says she was not crazy about them. She also loved comics such as *Wonder Woman* and *Batman*. Unknowingly, she had laid the necessary groundwork for her lifetime career as a writer, and the Steinem's way of living prepared her for the freelancer's life of boom and bust income.

Gloria does not blame her father for her self-education or the instability of always living on the edge of disaster. She credits him with her ability to dream, to make friends easily, and to find affection for non-domineering men because of her father's good-natured temperament. Since he became Gloria's primary caregiver while Ruth was infirm, he was more of a friend to her than a parent. The girls were always involved in the family business. Gloria was expected to wrap and unwrap the breakable antiques, which Leo would sell to dealers along the way, from the time when she was four years old. Leo bought Susanne a professional popcorn stand so that she could set up and sell treats at the beaches during winter months. And even as a child, he respected his children as people. Gloria always felt that he treated her as well as he treated himself.

A DRAMATIC CHANGE

In 1944, Ruth learned that Leo had mortgaged the pier and lake without her knowledge and, having had enough of his instability and constant financial games, insisted that she and Leo separate for at least one year. By this time, Susan was a junior at Smith College in Northampton, Massachusetts, a prestigious Seven Sisters college along with Barnard, Bryn Mawr, Mount Holyoke, Radcliffe, Vassar, and Wellesley. From among its stellar graduates have come the first woman to edit the *New York Times* business section, the first woman member of Johns Hopkins Medical School faculty, the first woman to head the White House Council of Economic Advisors, and the first woman to row the Atlantic alone. Smith has also produced Caldecott Medal winners for illustrated children's literature, Pulitzer Prize winners, and First Ladies of the United States. Ruth wanted to move closer to Susanne, and she and Gloria rented a small house in Amherst, Massachusetts, about nine miles from the college.

Ruth seemed to behave normally in their new surroundings. The house was neater, and, though Gloria missed her father, she loved her new home. The biggest reason was the relief she felt from playing mediator in her parents' squabbles over money. At 10 years old, Gloria finally felt as if her life had become normal. She learned to be with other kids, participated in group sports, such as softball, and went to school every day.

Gloria was in fifth grade by this time and felt lucky that the children at her new school welcomed her. She felt part of the group almost instantly and made up for the gaps in her knowledge by drawing on the information from the books she had read and her writing ability.

Ruth even had Gloria baptized in the Congregational Church while they were in Amherst. Yet, Gloria never ascribed to either her Jewish or Christian heritage. "I don't believe in either religion," she said. "When I'm around Jews who feel there's something good about being exclusively Jewish, I emphasize the non-Jewish side of the family. When I'm around Protestants, who think there's something good about being Protestant, then, I emphasize the Jewish side."[5] Although Gloria never felt that connected to her family, in Amherst she at least felt normal. But she had no way of knowing that this time was only a brief respite. It was, in fact, the end of her childhood.

As fifth grade ended, so did the term at Smith for Susanne. Susanne planned to hit Manhattan and work for Georg Jensen, a well-known artistic silver company, and Ruth and Gloria moved to Scarsdale, New York, to house-sit a home belonging to a friend of Ruth's from college. Susanne came from New York City to visit them most weekends, but generally Ruth and Gloria were alone, without even a car to transport them.

Even worse, Ruth fell back into her depression, complete with hallucinations. Gloria was left with utterly inadequate adult supervision, and there were no children in her neighborhood. She retreated once again into a world of books. She had no idea that this lonely summer was only a precursor to years that would test her character and strength.

ANOTHER SETTLEMENT

When the summer of 1944 ended, Ruth informed Gloria that they would move back to Toledo—to Ruth's family home—and, even at a time when the incidence of divorce was much lower than it would be in later years, Ruth announced that she would divorce Leo. Gloria was not as upset by the divorce as some children might have been. "My older sister, whose childhood years were those when my parents were happier with each other, was very upset by their divorce. I was more curious about why they had married than why they divorced. They were both good people but they didn't share many interests or values. I don't remember feeling sad or upset. [The divorce] seemed inevitable and better for everyone."[6] Gloria had found a happier life without the constant arguing around her. Yet, she was concerned about moving again, making new friends, going to new schools, and all that children worry about when their world is turned upside down. She had no clue that Toledo would be more than a new place to live. For her, it would be a long ordeal.

Before moving, the Steinems split their property equally; however, the resort on the property at Clark Lake (Ocean Beach) was not part of the bargain. When the business failed, due to wartime rationing, the furnishings and fixtures were sold at auction, and Leo literally had the resort blown up, but they still had joint ownership of the land and lake.

Ruth did not ask for alimony in the divorce settlement, at the behest of her attorney. She did not regard the gesture as giving up much, considering Leo's sporadic income. She approved of her lawyer's advice, seeing this waiver as a sign of independence.

Leo spoke to Gloria at the time and explained that he just was not able to handle Ruth's condition and the added stress of earning a living too.

His only means of support was through buying and selling antiques and collectibles, which involved traveling throughout the country to find and resell them. Gloria understood and never blamed him for the breakup. The characterization of Ruth and Leo's divorce as abandonment on the part of Leo still angers her. She recognized that her mother had left her father and that he had no choice but to continue to make a living the only way he could. She concluded that conducting his business and caring for Ruth simultaneously was impossible.

Leo continued to visit Gloria and Ruth each year when he came to town and sent them oranges from Florida. He even bought his daughters expensive gifts when he could afford it and once sent Gloria an expensive, soft, mouton (a sheepskin that is cut and processed to resemble seal or beaver) coat. Yet, sometimes when he came to visit, Ruth would not let him in the house.

Eventually, Leo married a Jewish woman from Germany who had tried to get a permanent visa for years. Leo apparently married her in order to assure her citizenship because they divorced not long after the marriage. Gloria never met the woman, although she once called Gloria many years later, claiming to be her stepmother, to ask if Gloria knew the whereabouts of Leo. The conversation ended quickly.

TOLEDO LIVING

Things did not go smoothly for Gloria and Ruth even after the divorce. Ruth had inherited her family home at 747 Woodville Road in East Toledo upon her parents' death, and the residence had been transformed into three apartments; however, tenants still resided in each of the units. So mother and daughter were forced to rent a basement apartment in West Toledo, which was the more desirable side of town.

Though Gloria liked the neighborhood, she was shocked at the small size of the apartment they had rented, which was constructed in a space behind the utility room in an old boardinghouse. To reach their combination living room-bedroom, they had to walk past an enormous boiler furnace. The kitchen and bathroom were situated even farther beyond, and they saw only car tires in the driveway through tiny windows. Since the living room-bedroom was too small for even single beds to sit side by side, Gloria and her mother slept in bunk beds, with Gloria on the top bunk and Ruth on the bottom.

Once they were settled, Gloria entered sixth grade at Monroe Elementary School after the school year had already begun. The kids in her class seemed to have progressed through the grades together, but Gloria had no trouble making friends. Her best friend lived in the boardinghouse upstairs, and they played together often. Sixth grade was also the year that Gloria got her first pair of eyeglasses, which made her feel grown up and somewhat attractive. She began to feel normal again just as the rug was about to be yanked away another time.

When school recessed for the summer, the tenant in the basement apartment of Ruth's house moved out and Ruth and Gloria prepared to move again. They had more space in the Woodville Road house, but the building was in terrible disrepair.

Before moving in, Ruth had suggested to the upstairs tenants, the Barnes family, that they move into the vacant downstairs apartment because it had more space. The upstairs had consisted of bedrooms and a hallway, and slanted rafters took much of the space, but it was enough room for Gloria and Ruth. The only drawback was that the kitchen sink had disappeared from the downstairs, so Ruth suggested that the Barnes family take the upstairs sink to replace it. Ruth never got a new sink for the upstairs kitchen.

Leo came to help Ruth and Gloria move their myriad boxes of belongings upstairs. Along with the Steinems came their dog, a chow chow named Ginger. For Gloria, two playmates were already built in—Marilyn and Lillian Barnes, one a year older and one a year younger than Gloria, who was by then 12 years old. Lillian instantly adulated Gloria because she seemed sophisticated and dressed more stylishly than other kids in the neighborhood.

However, the East Toledo surroundings did not suit Gloria at all; she felt like a stranger living in a bad dream. She remarked, "What I remember emotionally is the impact of suddenly realizing this was it. And the 'it' was quite depressing."[7] East Toledo was the wrong side of town.

LIFE ON THE OTHER SIDE OF THE TRACKS

In addition to the run-down condition of the house they lived in, the neighborhood suffered the permeating stench of automotive, shipbuilding, glass, meatpacking, and many other types of factory wastes, as Toledo was once a major business center. The rows of two-story houses on Woodville Road were better cared for than Ruth's, but constant truck traffic on the street in front of the house, which was situated on State Route 223, and glowing neon beer signs hanging on corner bars created a negative ambiance; and the people there seemed distressed and to be living day to day without hope of rising above their situation.

Neighborhood women were overwhelmingly mothers and housewives. Most of the men worked in factories or drove trucks; some were insurance agents or performed clerical functions. Few were well educated. Mr. Barnes, for example, had only completed third grade, and his wife had completed high school. Gloria felt not only the poverty but also the intellectual dearth, even at her young age.

The factory workers knew little about banking and checking accounts, as they were used to being paid and spending the cash, which was usually gone by the end of the week. What they could not pay for out of weekly wages was put on layaway, where people made cash payments until their stoves or Easter clothes were paid off and could be carried home. Gloria's mother was unusual in her neighborhood because she was a college graduate and had a checking account. Most often, due to her mother's mental state, Gloria would write the necessary checks out and have Ruth sign them.

To earn extra money, Gloria danced at the local Eagles and Elks clubs and got $10 a night for her talents. At one place, the stage was protected by chicken wire so that brawling drunks could not harm the performers with flying bottles and chairs. The macho environment of the town upset Gloria. She saw the people that lived around her as victims of life, living from week to week and looking forward to their Saturday night beer. She also knew that she and Ruth were part of it.

Shortly after moving to Woodville Road, Ruth's hallucinations became more pronounced. With great difficulty, Gloria convinced her to see a doctor—the same doctor from the sanatorium where she had stayed before Gloria was born, the only doctor Ruth ever trusted. After talking to her for only 20 minutes, the doctor informed Gloria that her mother should be institutionalized and admitted to a state hospital right away. Gloria remembered seeing horrible articles in magazines and newspapers about abuse and mishandling of patients in state hospitals.

Views on mental health problems in the 1950s differed from those of today. Institutions, often stumped by what to do for the mentally impaired, sometimes relied on shock treatments and even frontal lobe lobotomy for some patients; the drugs available to aid in the treatment of mental illness were not yet available. Radical procedures occurred at a higher rate in state-run institutions, and Gloria would never allow those things to happen to her mother. Living on the meager income that Ruth received from renting the apartments downstairs, what Gloria brought home from dancing, and a lease on Ruth's half of the land in Michigan, they could not afford a private hospital. Gloria felt there was no other option but to take her mother home. At 11 years old, Gloria assumed the role of mother and her mother became the child.

MOTHERING MOTHER

Gloria never asked for support from her relatives. Gloria's grandmother Marie occasionally came in to clean the house for them, all the while disdainful of their sloppy lifestyle. She and Ruth fought so much during Marie's visits that Marie eventually stopped coming.

Janey bought some of Gloria's clothes; Janey could afford clothes that Ruth never could. With a 1950s mentality about the illness Ruth suffered, Janey was somewhat disdainful of her sister. Janey viewed her illness as failing; they had been taught by their mother to aspire to middle-class life. Janey was not happy about having a crazy sister living on the wrong side of town. She saw Ruth as self-indulgent and weak and expected her to resolve to change her life for the better. Her pontificating ultimately lead to Ruth throwing Janey out of the house. Soon after, Gloria received a call from her aunt. She told Gloria to call in case of emergency but stated that she would never come back into the house.

Susanne had graduated from Smith and landed a job with Kay Associated Jewelry Stores. She traveled around the country giving educational talks about diamonds, having learned about the jewels through several geology courses and her stint with Georg Jensen in New York. She called Ruth and Gloria often and always came home for Christmas. Gloria always looked forward to her visits. After a call from Janey informing Susanne of the deplorable living conditions surrounding Ruth and Gloria, Susanne tried to get Ruth to move to Washington, D.C. The city was Susanne's current place of residence and she hoped that all three of them could live together, but continually Ruth refused.

Uncle Ed, Leo's brother who had strayed so far from the family's ideals, was helpful to Gloria and Ruth and kept their decrepit oil burner going in the winter. Yet, at 11, Gloria figured that the other relatives knew of her mother's condition and that they thought it was proper that she should be Ruth's caregiver. She took the onus for granted, accepted it, and lived life without complaint.

UNUSUAL CIRCUMSTANCES

On Thanksgiving weekend in 1947, when Gloria was in eighth grade, Ruth was convinced that World War II was going on outside their building and that the Nazis were coming to arrest them. She became highly agitated and put her fist through a window, hoping to escape. Her arm was badly cut. Gloria bandaged her wounds, sat beside her, and held her hand. Although she disapproved of her mother's addiction, she realized that administering the medication was unavoidable if she wanted to live even a seminormal life. She quickly administered the Doc Howard's medicine and waited for the remedy to do its best—put Ruth to sleep. Through the ordeal, she continued to hold Ruth with one hand and Dickens's *A Tale of Two Cities*, a class reading assignment, in the other. The reading may have helped her to remove herself from the situation, since only after Ruth dropped off was she able to submit to her own emotions of fear and desperation. Gloria loved her mother and wanted her to be well. The pain of knowing that would never happen and the anxiety over knowing such episodes were bound to arise again must have been almost too much for the child to bear.

Yet, Gloria was never able to find solace in her own home. Boxes that Leo had toted in for them were still packed, and aisles were created among them in order for people to walk. Sometimes in winter, Ruth and Gloria shared one bed for warmth, especially after the oil burner was ultimately red tagged and shut down by the Toledo Health Department. And Gloria's immature methods of housekeeping were less than perfect. Meals consisted of toast and coffee, bologna sandwiches, and lunchbox pies—young Gloria's version of a balanced diet. When all the dishes in the house were dirty, she put them into the bathtub and washed them because there was no kitchen sink.

Gloria's bedroom furniture consisted of a mattress and box spring on the floor and an old packing crate, which served as a closet. And in the living room, Gloria stacked books and papers to create two ersatz armchairs, when covered by blankets. The only other elements in the room were a rocking chair and a spinet piano.

During the day, Gloria practiced tap dancing on the bare floors to the complete dismay of the neighbors below her. Yet, she was determined to be a star. Sometimes, the neighbors would yell up and ask what she was doing, and Gloria would remind them that big stars had to practice.

But at night, there were rats. Ruth was indirectly responsible for their appearance; she had had an old garage with a collapsed roof torn down in the middle of winter. The rats had nowhere to go so they came into the house—in droves. They started in the basement and eventually made their way upstairs into both apartments.

Gloria was bitten one night, and Ruth summoned her courage to leave the house she never left to take her daughter to a hospital emergency room for treatment. This act touched Gloria, as it was the act of a normal mother, a mother Gloria wanted desperately. As an adult she wrote, "I feared that, if I allowed myself to feel the emotions this little girl had worked so hard to suppress... I would fall into an old and familiar well of invisibility and aloneness."[8]

NOTES

1. Quoted in Sydney Ladensohn Stern, *Gloria Steinem, Her Passions, Politics, and Mystique* (Secaucus, N.J.: Birch Lane Press, 1997), pp. 21–22.

2. Quoted on *The Fifties Web*, http://www.fiftiesweb.com/burma1.htm.

3. Cohen, *The Sisterhood*, p. 43.

4. Steinem, interview, 27 January 2003.

5. Cohen, *The Sisterhood.*, pp. 41–42.

6. Steinem, interview, 27 January 2003.

7. Quoted in Stern, *Gloria Steinem*, p. 35.

8. Steinem, *Revolution from Within*, p. 190.

Chapter 3

SALVATION AND DISCOVERY

Unlike most kids, Gloria did not play outside after school very often. She went home directly and carried her books into the house to check on her mother. Gloria always tried to keep her sense of humor, but it was difficult at times. The Doc Howard's medicine made Ruth's speech slurred, and people often mistook her for a drunkard. Ruth caused outlandish scenes, like the time she forgot that Gloria was at an after school activity and called the police, claiming that Gloria had disappeared. Gloria was mortified in front of her friends by the sirens and uniformed policemen who came to find her and take her home. At times like this, she sometimes blew up and ranted at her mother, who would apologize profusely. Seeing Ruth so fretful and contrite caused Gloria to regret that she had lost compassion as a result of her frustration with her mother's condition.

Throughout this time, when friends or other people asked why her mother acted so strangely, Gloria would simply reply in a quiet voice that Ruth was sick. But questions could only go so far with Gloria. Neighbor Lillian Barnes, who was the same age as Gloria, noticed that Gloria would put a quick halt to questions she deemed inappropriate: "She'd turn the switch off... I knew that if I went too far, Gloria would tell me to go to hell."[1]

Later, Gloria would summarize her mother's illness this way: "In retrospect, perhaps the biggest reason my mother was cared for but not helped for 20 years was the simplest: her functioning was not that necessary to the world."[2]

However, Ruth did have good periods. Once, she answered a classified ad to audition for an amateur acting troupe, and she and Gloria joined the cast in a production of *Noah's Ark*. Gloria acted onstage while Ruth shook metal sheets backstage to simulate thunder. And sometimes, Ruth could be cajoled into writing a small check for Gloria to cash so that she could go to the five and dime stores or to a movie, where she could escape the reality of her day-to-day life.

Once, when they lived in the basement apartment in West Toledo, Gloria even feigned illness, hoping to force Ruth into the role of mother. Yet, Ruth became even more depressed over her inability to assume it. Gloria later said, "I knew that my mother loved me, but that she couldn't take care of me."[3] From that time on, Gloria rarely got sick and learned to cope. There was nothing more to do.

Finding no comfort from adults inside her home, Gloria learned to depend on the kindness of others. Her favorite teacher in seventh grade was Miss Bruss, and she found some solace in her company and challenge in her teaching assignments: "She assigned us the task of copying a favorite painting—mine was a Degas scene of ballet dancers at the barre, for which I had absolutely no talent but she somehow got me to attempt it anyway. She also tried to civilize us enough to learn ballroom dancing."[4]

Inside her home that year, Gloria also solved the rat infestation problem by using traps and cages and, when the vermin were caught, by disposing of their bodies. She later said, "I believe it was from those little cages that I got the idea of having a cage myself. Because I so desperately wanted something safe to sleep in."[5] She never acted on this fantasy; however, she continued to seek the affection that she lacked at home in her relationships with others and felt safer outside than inside. Her relationship with Miss Bruss carried through seventh, eighth, and ninth grade, and of her teacher, Gloria remarked, "After school, she was also a Girl Scout leader, and I remember feeling safer and stronger with her."[6]

HIGH SCHOOL BEGINS

When Gloria started at Waite High School in 1948, she was friends with four girls. One girl was her best friend from elementary school, while the other three girls had come to Waite from a different school. They formed a secret sorority and named it Chi Alpha Tau. The association's rules required that members carry good grades and belong to other clubs. Initially, the club was exclusive to those five girls. But soon everyone wanted to join, and eventually the group decided to allow other members.

Gloria also took ballet lessons and by her junior year was dancing in junior concerts with the Toledo Orchestra. She also worked at the radio station, via a student internship, where she learned to read scripts and cue records. The experience landed her an after school job at a local radio station. She also worked at a clothing shop in downtown Toledo. From her sister, Gloria also learned about gems and impressed her friends with her expertise. She taught them the finer points of Theosophy as well and led her friends in discussions on the subject.

In addition to these intellectual pursuits, the girls all dressed alike, wearing sweaters, skirts, bobby socks, and brown penny loafers. Because her Aunt Janey bought most of her clothes and because she spent her after school earnings on lovely sweaters, Gloria clothes were always a bit nicer than the outfits her friends wore. Her knowledge, her clothes, and the fact that her sister had gone to Smith heightened her prestige among her peers. They knew no one who had gone to a Seven Sisters college. From the clothes she wore and her sophisticated demeanor, they assumed that Gloria came from an affluent family; she allowed few to visit her apartment.

In 1949 after Gloria's sophomore year began, President Harry S. Truman announced that the Soviet Union had exploded an atomic device. It was an announcement that shocked the American public. Since the nuclear explosions at Hiroshima and Nagasaki in Japan, which ended World War II, the Americans had complete domination of the atomic market. With this news of Soviet nuclear testing, Americans realized that our enemies might have the capability of sending a bomb to the United States—just as Japan had been bombed, causing horrible devastation—and the intensifying cold war suddenly became a major issue. The fear of nuclear war was firmly planted in American minds. Some people even built bomb shelters and stockpiled durable and emergency items such as canned goods, candles, water, and all it would take to survive until the nuclear fallout had passed. School children were routinely drilled for civil defense and were prepared to dive under desks or to retreat to protected hallways when bomb sirens sounded, although no building could protect them from the force of an atom bomb.

This fear of attack intensified with the Korean War, which began on June 25, 1950, when North Korean forces crossed the dividing line, established after World War II, and invaded South Korea. Soon the United States, anxious to control the spread of communism, jumped into the fray, and the cold war escalated as well as American alarm. Even after the Korean War ended, the possibility of nuclear war was still a clear and present danger to them.

However, life went on, and, by the end of the Korean conflict, radio, which had been the main source of entertainment for average Americans, was becoming less popular. Television had entered the social scene and was slowly taking over people's imaginations. Folks gathered in living rooms across America to enjoy shows such as the *Friday Night Fights* and the *Milton Berle Show*. Owning a television set was a luxury that not all Americans could afford.

Ruth and Gloria had no TV, but Gloria was satisfied with books and dancing. And there were still films at the theater with stars like Marlon Brando and Vivien Leigh in the 1951 production of Broadway's *A Streetcar Named Desire*, adapted by the play's author, Tennessee Williams. Shocking to many, the movie stretched the limits of censure standards for decency by including veiled references to prostitution and overt sexuality. For America, the world was changing; the weft of stern morality of earlier years was just beginning to unravel. No one at the time had any conception of the changes that were about to come, and teenaged Gloria continued to endure Toledo life.

WANTING A WAY OUT AND ULTIMATE SALVATION

In her sophomore year, Gloria planned to tap dance out of Toledo like Teresa Brewer, a pop singer of the 1950s and 1960s that had sung her way out of town via the same show for which Gloria auditioned. However, Gloria's tap dancing routine did not make the cut to be on *Ted Mack's Amateur Hour*. Still trying to break out, Gloria hoped that her tall, shapely physical stature and finely featured face would help her to win the Miss Capehart TV Contest, a beauty and talent contest that led to a national contest in Florida, far away from Toledo. She performed a Spanish dance complete with castanets but won runner-up. Her prize was a ruby and rhinestone necklace and earrings set, but not a ticket south.

Gloria had also tried to escape through religion. She received a white leather Bible for Christmas and began reading it daily. She also joined a Presbyterian church on the other side of town, though it took two street-cars[7] to attend services. No doubt, feeling that no one cared about her dire situation of living in poverty with a mentally unstable mother, Gloria found a sense of belonging and caring from the church.

But even a church could not solve all her problems. After the health department condemned their furnace, the Steinems could no longer rent the downstairs apartments for lack of heat. However, magically, a church did rescue Gloria from her miserable life. The Presbyterian church next door to her mother's house offered to buy her mother's property, intending to demolish the house and build a church annex on the site. Because Gloria was too young to make the decisions and Ruth was incapable of making them, the family came to Toledo to discuss the situation.

Susanne told her sister that she had a plan. She would ask her father Leo to take Ruth for one year so that Gloria could come to Washington, D.C., live with her, and complete her last year of high school there. Gloria was skeptical, and told Susanne that Leo would never go for the idea. Aside from being divorced, he would continue to remind them that it was impossible for him to make a living and care for Ruth too. Susanne was determined to ask him anyway.

In a restaurant at breakfast the next morning, Leo reacted just as Gloria had expected, and Susanne stormed out in anger. With the problem still unresolved, Leo and Gloria just sat looking at each other for a few moments, and then Gloria reminded her father that she had to go to work. In the car, she said nothing and felt no hostility. She believed that Ruth was not Leo's responsibility; she did not see that it was his lifestyle and the constant anxiety that Ruth was forced to endure in their marriage that had driven Ruth into a depression in the first place. In that respect, Ruth could be considered his responsibility too.

Upon Gloria's arrival at work, she opened the car door and burst into tears; and Gloria never cried. Leo was astonished and so was she. Her tears softened his heart and he agreed to take Ruth, but only for one year. After that, she would be the girls' responsibility again. Gloria remembers him telling her to synchronize her watch because he would give Ruth back one year after that day.

Ruth set aside the $8,000[8] from the sale of her house so that Gloria could go to college and went off to travel with Leo. In her mind, they were not divorced because they had been married twice but had divorced only once; so she believed their relationship was still proper.

Gloria and Susanne packed up the house and set off for Georgetown, an historic section of western Washington, D.C. It was the end of Gloria's torment and one important turning point in her life. Although Gloria would not be financially set for years to come, she would never live in abject poverty again and she would never be her mother's sole caretaker again.

A NEW LIFE

Like Cinderella, 17-year-old Gloria was suddenly set free of her bondage and ready to try on the glass slipper. She was eager to move to Georgetown, where her sister lived with two other roommates. However,

Susanne's friends were hesitant to have another girl living in the house, especially one so much younger than they were—a high school girl. When Susanne offered to get rid of her own chow chow dog, which one of the roommates barely tolerated, they reluctantly agreed to allow Gloria stay.

All three older women had careers. Susanne was 26 and on her way to becoming a certified gemologist. She even had her own local television show, *Gem Session*, and the other two girls worked full-time. Their quasi-indignant attitudes toward Gloria made her uncomfortable. Aside from her anxiety over starting a new high school, she knew that Susan's roommates saw her as a crasher.

Still, they felt sorry for her because she was still young and away from her mother. They did not realize how happy Gloria really was to be free. However, during this Washington period, she had distance and time to assess her mother's illness. She wrote, "I began to think about the many pressures that might have led up to that first nervous breakdown."[9] Ruth had to leave Susanne with her grandmother, whose values she did not hold; she had to give up her job at the newspaper, which she loved; and she almost died in a miscarriage, mishandled by her own mother. The distance helped Gloria to understand her mother but not to miss taking care of her, which had been an enormous burden for the past 11 years.

Georgetown was the nicest place in which Gloria had ever lived. With its western boundary on the Potomac River, Georgetown has always retained its own character, apart from the District of Columbia. The elegant quarter of stone and brick residences, dating as far back as 1765, include Georgian mansions and townhouses, federal and classical revival houses, and more ornate homes that date back to ante- and postbellum periods. Yet, the Victorian row houses, which sit side by side with a common wall, are the district's mark.

Georgetown is also a college town, the home of Georgetown University, the nation's oldest Catholic university. Washington, D.C., also boasts other renowned schools, including American University, George Washington University, and Loyola College. Although her formal schooling had been sporadic in her youth, Gloria's reading made her more aware of the world than many of her well-schooled peers. Her long division might have been sketchy, but her knowledge was vast. Georgetown was just the type of environment where Gloria would tend to flourish.

Often, to get away from the apartment that summer, Gloria swam at a nearby hotel that charged nonresidents to use the facility. She met other people there and, one day, agreed to a date with a naval officer almost twice her age. When she brought him to the apartment, Susan's room-mates quickly changed their attitudes toward Gloria. If she could date men closer to their ages, they would have to rethink their attitudes about her maturity.

Gloria would later claim that Georgetown was the first place where she realized that people ate regular meals around a table, rather than while standing in front of the refrigerator. Her high school in Georgetown was also the first place she went to that was an upscale school. Western High School (now Duke Ellington School of the Arts) was considered to have such high academic standards that students from nearby communities paid tuition to attend, though it was a public school. The student body included children of congressmen, diplomats, and military personnel. And as with most learning institutions throughout the country, there was still racial segregation. Western was an all-white school, unlike the school Gloria had attended in Toledo.

TRANSFORMATION OF GLORIA AND THE AMERICAN LIFESTYLE

This state of events, however, was about to change. On February 28, 1951, *Brown vs. the Board of Education of Topeka* was filed in a federal district court when Oliver Brown sued the local school board for making his daughter walk a mile to school when white children were bussed to a school only a few blocks away. Ultimately, in 1954, the Supreme Court would hear the case and unanimously strike down the concept of separate but equal in biracial communities; they declared segregation a violation of the Fourteenth Amendment to the U.S. Constitution, which states:

> All persons born or naturalized in the United States, and subject to the jurisdiction thereof, are citizens of the United States and of the state wherein they reside. No state shall make or enforce any law which shall abridge the privileges or immunities of citizens of the United States; nor shall any state deprive any person of life, liberty, or property, without due process of law; nor deny to any person within its jurisdiction the equal protection of the laws.[10]

With this development, the African American struggle, not only for desegregation but also for equality in all areas of American life, would begin. At the time of this momentous initial action on the part of Brown and the NAACP, Gloria and most other young white people in America were oblivious to the changes headed for America. Still living in their own worlds of teenage angst, daily life went on.

Gloria was fortunate to find that her anxiety over attending yet another new school was unfounded. Due to the makeup of the student body and the professions of their parents, students came and went regularly. Gloria remembered, "Many of those at Western came from military families who moved constantly."[11] The student body was not as static as those of most American schools. The makeup at Western was constantly changing, and students there were quite accepting of new students. Gloria fit right in, and the best sororities on campus urged her to join. She chose the sorority considered the best on campus—Zeta Beta Psi.

Gloria's classmates considered her to be serious and perceived her aura of maturity. One of them remarked, "Gloria had a social conscience before there was a word for it."[12]

Although Gloria had spent the past six and a half years acting the adult and dealing with issues such as paying the bills, doing laundry, and grocery shopping while caring for Ruth, she still had gaps in her knowledge base to conceal. Outwardly she appeared to be confident and mature, while inside, she was apprehensive.

The cure for Gloria was to throw herself into various school activities. That year, she was elected vice president of both the senior class and the student council. She joined the archery club and was secretary of the French club, among other honors and functions. She was also chosen for the Miss Western contest sponsored by the school newspaper, the *Western Breeze*.

Soon Gloria was going steady with one of the school's most preferred dates. Although many of the guys wanted to date Gloria, he was one of few who had the courage to ask her. She was not only attractive, but other Western students respected her for her intellect and quick wit.

PLOTTING FOR THE FUTURE

Popular Gloria was not one of the top students at Western; however, she was a hard worker. Her SAT scores were 640 in verbal and 484 in math, out of a possible 800 for each. Yet, her score of 675 on the English achievement test would get her into Smith—that, and the fact that she was a legacy, owing to Susanne's graduation from the school. Before she was accepted by Smith, Gloria applied to Stanford and Cornell as well. Her guidance counselor at Western and her vice-principal both wrote recommendations to Smith for her, since it was Gloria's school of choice. Their recommendations were just the touch she needed, and Gloria was thrilled by her acceptance. She would go to Smith and major in political science. When she graduated from Western on June 12, 1952, she looked forward to her new college adventure.

Yet, she anticipated her matriculation with hesitance. She met another girl who was headed for Smith, and the girl was extremely wealthy—the type who had an open-ended credit card and used it to hire limousines. Gloria worried that she would not fit in among the rich women at Smith, while Susanne tried to console her. She had been to Smith and assured her sister that on campus none of that mattered. Her high school yearbook entry declared that "Glo" would be "a sure success at Smith."[13]

Around the same time that Gloria graduated, Leo's year of caring for Ruth was up. They had traveled as much as they had during the years when the family would travel from Clark Lake. Now Ruth became Susanne's problem. Ruth joined Susanne and Gloria in a three bedroom house that Susanne had rented for them that summer; but come September, Gloria would go off to Smith, while Ruth would be left in Susanne's care.

Gloria worried that Susanne would not be able to care for their mother. Six years of dealing with Ruth's irrational behavior made Gloria the expert; Susanne had no idea how bizarre Ruth's actions could be. When Susanne had visited them in Toledo, Ruth had tried to maintain a semblance of normalcy. She did not seem quite so frail or needy at those times, was more charming, and enjoyed receiving gifts. There had never been panic attacks or outlandish behavior while Susanne was visiting.

SMITHWARD BOUND

Gloria eventually accepted Susanne's prodding and got onto the train bound for Northampton, Massachusetts, the home of Smith College. Susanne went with her to make sure that Gloria settled into her old dormitory, Laura Scales (housing around 70 girls from all economic backgrounds), and then returned to Washington, D.C. Gloria found herself in one of the more modern buildings on campus, as it had been built in 1936, only two years after she was born. One of 10 houses on the quad, Laura Scales is red brick and massive, with white window trimming, white columns, and a cupola, in the American classical revival style. The building has single rooms on three floors and joins the Franklin King house through a communal dining room. The two buildings form a semicircle, which encloses a small courtyard, the scene of Smith's annual commencement proceedings.

The campus consists of 125 acres of beautiful landscaping, with manicured tree lined streets. Ivy covered structures, ranging from Gothic to colonial to modern architectural styles, the lake called Paradise Pond; the conservatory (with a new glasshouse going up that year); and a small waterfall at Allen Field add to the collegiate ambiance that promotes a pensive atmosphere. Yet, only a few hundred yards away are the streets of downtown Northampton, offering stores and restaurants familiar to city life.

One of Gloria's first acts upon arriving at Smith was to peruse the orientation handbook for freshmen. She learned that Bermuda shorts two inches above the knee were acceptable, as were jeans, but at dinner the women were expected to wear skirts and sweaters. Also popular were knee socks and button down shirts, once belonging to girls' fathers, even with frayed collars and cuffs.

But Smith's roots and philosophy did not focus on charm and grace. Sophia Smith, who founded the school in her last will and testament of 1870, declared:

> I hereby make the following provisions for the establishment and maintenance of an Institution for the higher education of young women, with the design to furnish for my own sex means and facilities for education equal to those which are afforded now in our colleges to young men.
>
> It is my opinion that by the higher and more thorough Christian education of women, what are called their wrongs will be redressed, their wages adjusted, their weight of influence in reforming the evils of society will be greatly increased, as teachers, as writers, as mothers, as members of society, their power for good will be incalculably enlarged.[14]

Sophia Smith had plans for Smith College to supersede girls' schools, which concentrated primarily on domesticity and instruction in traditionally feminine careers, such as nursing, teaching, or library science. She wanted to change the landscape of society, not so much by providing women with an education that would enable them to compete with men on a level playing field, but more so by enabling them to be better wives and mothers. Even at this end, the idea of such stilted endeavors put Sophia Smith ahead of her time.

THE RED SCARE

However, a cloud of uncertainty hung over the school by the time Gloria arrived. The red scare—American fear of Communism and communist infiltration in the United States government and other institutions—began around the time of the Bolshevik victory in Russia and was reawakened soon after the end of World War II.

In 1950, when Wisconsin Senator Joseph McCarthy raised accusations claiming members of the State Department had ties to communism, he came to the forefront of the investigations as chairman of the Senate Permanent Investigations Committee. McCarthy raised the already present fear of communism, and Americans began to fear not only an attack from without, but also that there was disloyalty from within. McCarthy's committee investigated many people from all sectors, but especially those involved in the entertainment industry, who were suspected of providing communist propaganda. His dogged search for signs of the red menace lead to the term McCarthyism, and under his intense scrutiny, many were not only tagged as communists, but also ruined.

Academia came under examination, however, in the late 1940s, when the Truman administration was pressured by right-wing groups, such as the National Council for American Education and the Anti-Communist League of America, to wash communist sympathizers out of schools across the country. In 1949, the House Un-American Activities Committee (HUAC) began inspecting books for communist messages, and the National Education Association voted to ban communist members from its roles.

People were coerced into signing loyalty oaths, which gave the Civil Service Commission of the federal government the right to investigate them and disavowed any ties to the Communist Party. Oaths were required of teachers in 36 states by 1951, and the penalty for not signing the oath was termination of employment and disgrace. Suspected communists were placed on a permanent blacklist and could not regain employment. One academician remarked, "Scores of scholars were not only driven from their universities but from their profession, sought refuge abroad, even gave up scholarship entirely. Institutes were closed, journals collapsed, books were censored."[15]

When Smith fell under the anticommunist microscope, the students were in an uproar, and no one was more furious than Gloria. As a result, her anger developed an interest in Marxism that she would court until a few years later.

NOTES

1. Cohen, *The Sisterhood*, p. 49.

2. Steinem, *Outrageous Acts*, p. 149 (reprint ed.).

3. Quoted in Stern, *Gloria Steinem*, p. 24.

4. Gloria Steinem, interview with author, 2 February 2003.

5. Quoted in Stern, *Gloria Steinem*, p. 43.

6. Steinem, interview, 2 February 2003.

7. Streetcars were a common form of public transportation. Although similar to buses, they are powered differently. Streetcars run on rails via electrical current rather than on wheels powered by a gasoline engine.

8. In 2003, the amount would have been worth about $140,000 (when compared to the Gross Domestic Product (GDP) per capita of that year).

9. Steinem, *Outrageous Acts*, p. 155.

10. U.S. Constitution, amend. 14, sec. 1.

11. Steinem, interview, 2 February 2003.

12. Quoted in Stern, *Gloria Steinem*, p. 59.

13. "Gloria Marie Steinem," Photo archive, *District of Columbia Public Schools*, http://www.k12.dc.us/dcps/graphics/gallery/Gloria_Steinem.jpg.

14. "Last Will and Testament of Miss Sophia Smith, Late of Hatfield, Mass.," *Five Colleges Digital Archives Project*, 1870, http://clio.fivecolleges.edu/smith/ss-wills/1870/transcript.htm.

15. C. Vann Woodward, "Academic Freedom: An Analysis of Two Breaches," *Academic Questions*, Fall 1997, pp. 71–74.

Chapter 4

ON A NEW TRACK

Gloria entered college when the country hated communists and feared the atom bomb, and every institution, church, and school operated under the 1950s atmosphere of traditional feminine suppression. Gloria once remarked, "The goal of the education was very often stated…'If we are ever to have educated children, we have to have educated mothers.'"[1] The mores of that era virtually dictated that even college educated women were not preparing for a career, but for marriage and raising children.

Although many of the students wore enormous engagement diamonds to class, Smith was a school for everyone. A 1922 New York *Evening Post* article remarked of the typical novice student: "She is positively welcomed by the whole college. Welcomed, that is, into the home and social life of the place…. They take her into the life of the house and of the college immediately…. With all allowances made. Smith College seems a very good place for the normal, self-reliant, responsible, conscientious American girl."[2]

Gloria found herself at home at Smith and she was accepted, despite her roots in Toledo poverty. In her freshman year, she took classes in English, French, geology, theater, and gym. French and geology were difficult for her. To help her with French, she enlisted the help of a classmate, Nancy Howard, who had been taught by a private tutor before entering Smith. In return, Gloria taught Nancy how to put on makeup, which Nancy had never worn before then.

Gloria, who had never been interested in science, decided to take geology because she saw it as the least scientific science. Once, on a field trip for the course, she saw a large turtle that had crawled up from a riverbank and seemed about to meander into traffic. Gloria took the turtle back to the edge of the water with some difficulty. As she placed it in the water, her teacher came up and told her that the turtle had probably spent a long time crawling up the bank to lay its eggs, and that she had just put it back into the water. "Well, I felt terrible," she said. "But in later years, I realized that this was the most important political lesson I learned, one that cautioned me about the authoritarian impulse of both left and right—always ask the turtle."[3]

Not only was Gloria bad at geology, she was equally bad, if not worse, at physical education. She once remarked, "If there were an Olympic team for sitting still, I would be on it."[4] Never having been a physical type as a child, she had no experience with sports such as tennis, volleyball, or golf, so she merely suffered through the required two years of the class. Her major phys ed accomplishment was obtaining a junior lifesaving badge in swimming, which she was later able to put to good use.

Other classes were not so painful. Government was her favorite class and she enjoyed philosophy. She was also a natural writer. One writing instructor told her that she should follow her talent, and she kept the idea in the back of her mind.

Another of Gloria's gifts was charming the girls with whom she lived. Gloria was different from other Smith girls. Her years as a dancer influenced her graceful movements, and she kept her fingernails long and manicured. She even wore eye makeup when none of the other Smith girls did, and she wore jeans, while they wore Bermuda shorts. To many of them, she seemed elegant, like someone to admire and emulate.

Gloria was also fun. She taught her friends how to knit and one girl, who had been raised by an English nanny and had never cared for garments, how to iron. She liked to talk with her dorm sisters late into the night and was a good listener. Her imagination and quick intellect spawned one-act plays from one-word prompts. Even the professors liked her and often invited her to tea or dinner. Although she dated other men, Gloria continued to date her high school boyfriend throughout her freshman year and visited him at West Point Military Academy in New York for Christmas.

In 1952, poet and author Sylvia Plath was another well-respected member of the student body. She earned top grades in all her classes and had published her first work at the age of eight. Her excellence earned her the position of guest editor for *Mademoiselle* magazine's special college edition that summer, a position that proved to be too stressful for her. Before entering her junior year at Smith, Plath wrote in her journal, "You walked in laughing, tears welling confused, mingling in your throat. How can you be so many women to so many people, oh you strange girl?"[5] Soon after, Plath suffered a nervous breakdown, tried to commit suicide by swallowing a handful of pills, and landed in a hospital for psychiatric treatment. She would return to Smith and graduate summa cum laude, Phi Beta Kappa in 1955, although life would never be easy for such a talented, sensitive spirit as hers, and she would end her own life in February 1963 at the age of thirty.

SECOND YEAR WOES AND EXCITEMENT

When Gloria's sophomore year began in September 1953, her financial situation was tight. Although her tuition had been paid from the proceeds of the sale of her mother's Toledo house, she still waited banquet tables, when possible; applied for a small scholarship; and sought to borrow money from the college for other expenses of living away from home. The amount she needed was less than $1,000.[6] Leo also contributed when he could, but his aid was erratic.

Economics aside, as her sophomore year wound down, Gloria was well entrenched in Smith society, and she and her dorm friends labeled themselves the Twelve Foolish Virgins, with economic backgrounds spanning wealthy to wanting.

In that second year, Gloria had also realized that she could study in Switzerland for $1,800—the same tuition that she would pay at Smith for one year—and jumped at the chance to see Europe. Her application was accepted in March 1954, as 1 of 52 students who would study abroad.

But before she left, she had a busy summer. That year, she used her lifesaving badge from Smith to get a job as a lifeguard at an inner-city pool in Washington, D.C. Though she was not the athletic type, she enjoyed the atmosphere, and the patrons found her interesting, as the only white person at the pool. Yet, she fit in. The pool regulars even taught her to play bones (an informal musical instrument played by slapping two clappers or spoons together and against the palms of the hands, legs, and body to create a rhythmic sound).

Also that summer, Gloria's sister married Robert Patch, a patent attorney, and Gloria was Susanne's maid of honor. Both parents attended the wedding.

Ruth had spent some months in a psychiatric hospital the year before and then returned to live with Susanne and her new husband, but only briefly. Ruth rented an apartment in northwest Washington, D.C., and got a job in a hotel gift shop. She seemed to be living a somewhat normal life. With events settled at home, Gloria set off to see the world. Next stop—Paris.

OFF TO EUROPE

Upon the day of Gloria's departure for Europe, in the fall of 1954, Ruth, Susanne, and Susanne's new husband, Bob, traveled to New York to see Gloria off on the ocean liner *Queen Elizabeth*. Decked out in her Cunard lines livery of black hull, white superstructure, and orange funnels with black tops, the ship resembled others that will go down in history, such as the *Lusitania*, the *Brittanic*, and the *Carparthia*, which rescued the survivors of the ill-fated *Titanic*. Cunard's *Queen Elizabeth* was the largest passenger vessel of her day. Used as a troop transport ship during World War II, the *Queen Elizabeth* had only been refitted and taken her maiden passenger voyage eight years earlier.

The ship was decorated in an elegant style, reminiscent of the art deco period of the 1920s and 1930s. Included in her amenities were a swimming pool, a restaurant, and Turkish baths. She would make the transatlantic crossing in less than a week. Although the 12 Smith girls who sailed with Gloria were crowded three or four to a cabin, they managed to enjoy having their baths drawn by the ship's stewards, even though they were traveling second class.

When they arrived in Paris, the students lived with French families and studied intensively with Mademoiselle Oiseau, with whom they visited and learned much about the city. Their teacher described the historic sights of Paris, complemented their lessons in phonetics and grammar, and provided them with instruction in the culture and customs of the country; and she did it all in French. The girls also had lessons in literature and medieval art. Daily, this occurred between nine and half past twelve, at which time they would break for lunch and then resume.

After six weeks, they departed for Geneva, in western Switzerland, where they would spend the balance of their year abroad, studying at the University of Geneva. Unlike the sleepy town of Northampton where the girls could wear shorts to class, they would be expected to dress in business formal and wear suits, dresses, and high-heels. Although this seemed a bit stuffy for the Smith coeds, it was a mild price to pay to be living and studying in Switzerland.

The Swiss canon of Geneva has a long history, as it has been inhabited for the past 12,000 years. The area provides a moderate climate, with average temperatures ranging from 36° to 74° Fahrenheit, and offers numerous museums, concert halls, theaters, and art galleries. In the eighteen century, Geneva became a banking center; the city has also become well-known for watch making and for its artisans, who toil in delicate enamel work. Famous former residents of the city include philosophers and authors Jean Jacques Rousseau, Francois Marie Arouet (known as Voltaire), and Henry Dunant, who established the International Committee of the Red Cross there in 1864. Geneva was also the home of the League of Nations after World War I.

Many of the Smith students lived in a small hotel on Lake Geneva, where they occupied most of the rooms. A history professor from Smith College, Elisabeth Kafka, accompanied the girls and lived in the hotel with them. Each night they gathered in a private dining room to discuss the events of the day.

During that first semester, they learned a great deal of German history from Professor Kafka, international law from Professor Bourquin, international migrations, modern French literature, comparative constitutional law, history of European civilization, and questions of international history. However, Gloria wrote to her mother that the courses were not up to American university standards. She thought them entirely too focused, pinpointing one facet of a subject rather than delving into its fundamental nature.

LIVING LIKE A NATIVE

Eventually, a few students were selected to live with Swiss families, Gloria among them. Her family lived on the other side of the lake, and the distance from the other Smith students caused her to feel isolated. She was so far from the university that she had to take public transportation to and from her classes, which was slightly intimidating since she was still not highly fluent in French.

Gloria consoled herself by eating Swiss chocolates and ice cream and added weight, until she was 150 pounds. Although the girls thought her figure was voluptuous, she felt ashamed at going down the road of her father, who was 300 pounds by that time, and vowed to never again allow her weight to get out of control. She never has.

For her second semester, Gloria moved back in with the other students and soon attracted men of all types. Her classmates remember that she was not discriminating and would go out with almost anyone who asked. Although Gloria's behavior was not in tune with the mores of the 1950s, she still worried about pregnancy and therefore had no serious relationships, although she had lost her virginity in 1953 at age 19. She says this happened with a "wonderful person," to whom she was very attracted.[7]

One major concern for any sexually active woman in the 1950s was avoiding pregnancy. The birth control pill had yet to be developed and women had to use diaphragms, intrauterine devices (IUDs), spermicides, and closely monitor the rhythm of their bodies. Ovulation time was definitely not a good time to have sex. Condoms were also available, but, like today, they were not 100 percent effective, nor were the other options. Pregnancy out of wedlock could ruin a girl for life and it was at the forefront of every mature woman's mind.

Gloria's short-term relationships seemed to feed her appetite for affection, which she craved in her childhood. The most meaningful relationship for her in Geneva was with a young Indian teaching assistant from one of her courses. The professor who taught that class, on communism, was completely chauvinistic when it came to female students. Yet, he thought Gloria's paper on the Indian Communist Party was the best he had seen and thought it should be published after Gloria adjusted the text. She knew that her lover had contributed to getting the professor's attention toward her work and to the paper's success.

This term paper not only earned her a good grade, but it also changed her philosophies and her interest in Marxism. She came to realize, through her work, that Marxism on paper and Marxism in practice were very different. The initial Indian Communist Party had neglected to include the middle-class landowners and the peasant-caste proletariat when they organized the movement; therefore, they negated a segment of the population even though communism was intended to be complete. She saw this as a pitfall in the overall ideology and began to rethink her views on Marxist philosophy.

ISSUES AT HOME

At the same time in America, Gloria was elected president of her dorm, Laura Scales. Although it was an honor, the news did not please her. She knew that if Smith did not agree to give her the scholarship she had applied for to complete her senior year, she would have to move into another dorm, where the students did the housework in exchange for a lower cost of living. By the time her message got back to Smith to decline the nomination, the election had already been held and she had won. She sent back a letter, regretfully turning down the office.

She did, in fact, receive news thereafter that her scholarship had been declined and she was furious, an unlikely state for Gloria to assume, as she is generally easygoing and rarely loses her temper. When she does, the situation is serious. In this case, she wrote to her mother: "All of this makes me just a little angry, especially in the light of Smith's 'generous' offer to loan me the 900 and let me pay it back after I graduate."[8] Gloria found it ludicrous that the school could encourage her to apply for a myriad of fellowships and still saddle her with a $900 debt. She also pointed out that three girls in the Geneva group, who were obviously well-off and not at all good students had been given aid, and told her mother that she would not see Ruth working at minimum wage to keep her in school. She decided that she would have to tell Smith she was dropping out to attend George Washington University in Washington, D.C. Yet, by the end of summer, Gloria won top grades and added recommendations from Mme. Kafka, which led to Smith College's reversal of their decision on Gloria's scholarship. Smith would provide the funds necessary for her to remain at Laura Scales.

As her school year in Geneva ended, Gloria applied for a course on politics and literature in the twentieth century at Oxford University in England for the summer, as she wanted to continue her time in Europe. With help from Leo to pay living expenses and a scholarship for the course, she added the money she had scrimped together and paid for her summer in England. At the end of that period, she joined a friend in a cycling tour of Scotland, which was agonizing due to the hilly terrain, but she enjoyed herself nonetheless. Soon after, she visited all the sites in England that she could, imagining she would never see Europe again.

Gloria was anxious to begin her senior year studies in September 1955; however, she had decided to honor in government. This required higher academic standards: a minimum 3.3 grade point average in major courses; two extra credit hours in the major; and a thesis with an oral exam based on its contents. It also required a recommendation from the department; more independent study, with fewer classes; and a heavier workload. Gloria's thesis was "Humanist and Ideologue," in which she compared the politics of British authors George Orwell (*1984*, published in 1949; *Animal Farm*, published in 1945) and Arthur Koestler (*Darkness at Noon*, published in 1940; *The Ghost in the Machine*, published in 1967), both social philosophers. Gloria had been elected Phi Beta Kappa, due to her major in liberal arts, completion of 90 semester hours in liberal arts and sciences, and a 3.65 or higher grade point average. Obviously, by the end of her junior year, Gloria was a top Smith student.

Also that fall, a college friend, who had dropped out to marry, invited Gloria to spend a weekend in Westchester County, New York, just north of New York City. There she met Blair Chotzinoff and was immediately attracted to him. "He had dark hair, dark skin, and greenish eyes," she said.[9] He had worked for the daily newspaper, the *New York Post*, for a time, and the two had their interest in writing in common.

She was further impressed when he flew her back to Northampton in a rented Piper Tripacer airplane and landed it on Smith's croquet field. They laughed and carried on for the entire flight and, by the end of it, they were equally smitten.

TO BE OR NOT TO BE?

Blair was 28, while Gloria was still only 21 years old. Aside from his higher maturity level than boys Gloria's age, Blair also came from an interesting family, as she came to learn upon visiting his family in Ridgefield, Connecticut. His maternal uncle was world-renowned violinist Jascha Heifetz, and his father was classical pianist, writer, and critic Samuel Chotzinoff, known as Chotzie to his friends. The family rounded out with the mother, Pauline, who was very beautiful and had appeared on Broadway, and Blair's 25-year-old sister, Anne, who was referred to as Cookie.

By that time, the senior Chotzinoff was music director of the National Broadcasting Company (NBC) and a well-known music critic. He had created the NBC Orchestra for Arturo Toscanini, the famous Italian conductor, who led the orchestra in several televised concerts between 1937 and 1954. Although the Chotzinoffs were not fabulously wealthy, they traveled in circles of well-known people in the music world, and Gloria once met conductor Leonard Bernstein through the Chotzinoffs.

Blair had spent much of his youth dating starlets and strippers, and Gloria was certainly a social improvement; yet, his parents were not as enthusiastic about her as Blair had become in a short time. They disagreed with her political views and were stunned when she had the gumption to argue with Blair's father. The Chotzinoffs considered Gloria, coming from poverty, to be a social climber, which she understandably was, wanting to erase the stigma of life in Toledo while the Chotzinoffs thought she was looking for money, expensive gifts, and a good time. To boot, Gloria was only half Jewish, and the fact that the Chotzinoffs were intent on their son's wife being 100 percent Jewish made her stress her Christian heritage, as she never wanted to be classified by religion.

Regardless of his parents' feelings, Blair and Gloria spent every week-end together that they could, and a torrid love affair continued. Although Blair was not Gloria's first sexual partner, she considered this to be her first meaningful relationship; but because the couple was still not established personally or financially, the relationship's tenure was doubtful.

Blair flew airplanes for the National Guard out of Purchase, New York, but was between jobs and broke. Gloria was always strapped for money, but the two enjoyed just being together and now and then scraping up enough for a romantic dinner.

At 22 years of age, Gloria agreed to Blair's proposal of marriage, and he gave her a huge diamond. Yet, the engagement did not last long, as Gloria was not ready to marry—not then and perhaps not ever, and she told him so and gave back his ring. Blair raced to Northampton, they had a tearful reconciliation, and, by the end of the evening, Blair and Gloria were reengaged.

Although Gloria had severe reservations about marriage, it had little or nothing to do with Blair himself. In 1956, it was customary for women to marry and have a home and a family. They were expected to be Betty Crocker, Suzy Homemaker, or like TV mom icons—Mrs. Cleaver of *Leave It to Beaver* and Margaret Anderson of *Father Knows Best*—that typified the ideal 1950s wife and mother, though few could match their even tempers and their perfect ways. The outright choice to remain single was highly unusual, suspect to speculation about a woman's sexual orientation, and even a bit outrageous. Women who did not marry, even by choice, were referred to as spinsters and old maids. Gloria saw the determination to marry as the last selection a woman was able to make.

A majority of married women did not work, even part-time. Following the nine-to-five routine was a husband's purpose in life, and most men thought it a blow to their masculinity to have their women in regular jobs. Not only were women considered masculine possessions, after they said, "I do," to the ceremonial love, honor, and obey, but also after marriage, most choices, perhaps aside from what color to choose for the kitchen curtains, were the husband's domain. He decided where the couple lived, how the money was spent, and expected a hot meal on the table and clean, scrubbed children when he got home from work every day. A married woman in a regular nine-to-five job was shocking, and everyone, including the women themselves, saw a wife's sole responsibility as keeping the house and children.

Gloria saw that commitment meant losing power over her own life. She had seen her parents' marriage end in divorce and the mental infir-

mity of her mother that was caused by never living the life she had anticipated. Gloria never wanted to fall into that trap nor did she want to be
tethered to any man. Even more than that, she did not want to mother
anyone, as she had had enough of caring for someone else, having cared
for her own mother. Having children meant assuming that role all over
again. Avoiding marriage actually made Gloria feel more secure and in
control of her own life. Yet, she truly loved Blair. Her approach to avoid
spending the rest of her life with him and to avoid following social con-
ventions of the time, coupled with her love for Blair, was terribly confus-
ing.

GOING THROUGH THE MOTIONS

Gloria's Smith friends held a bridal shower for her once they learned
she had become engaged. Although touched by their generosity, Gloria
remained detached throughout the party. For some reason, she felt as
though she was watching the entire shower from a distance.

Around that same time, Gloria began to consider her future and weigh
possible careers for herself. She consulted her guidance counselor at
Smith and asked about the possibilities of attending law school; she was
quickly discouraged. The counselor advised her that women with law degrees were consigned to the position of law research rather than the practice of law.

With that option abandoned, Gloria began writing. She published several book reviews in the Smith student newspaper, the *Sophian,* and decided that she might work toward getting a job in the publishing industry.

Her first interview was with *Time* magazine; however, they would not
hire women writers, only women researchers. She applied for the position
of copywriter at advertising agencies, but was told she was not suited for
the position. No job that appealed to her was accepting women, and as a
backstop her engagement continued.

Gloria's parents had mixed reactions to Gloria's impending marriage.
Blair and Ruth got along very well. In fact, Ruth told Gloria to get married right out of college. "Or," she said, "once you get a taste of being independent, you'll never want to get married."[10] However, Leo was
indifferent. If Gloria wanted to get married, it was fine with him, but, as
he had become a gem expert over the years through his dealing with antique jewelry, he advised Gloria that the diamond in her engagement ring
was yellow and therefore less valuable. This downgraded Blair in Leo's
eyes.

When her senior year ended, Gloria was sad to leave Smith, her first secure home. She was elected as class historian and wrote an essay about matrimony versus career for the *Alumnae Quarterly* magazine. Poet Archibald MacLeish spoke at the commencement, attended by Ruth, Leo, and Susan, and MacLeish urged the graduates to seek change.

SUMMER LEADS TO SANCTUARY

Gloria's life turned yet again when she left Smith. She went back to Washington, D.C., for the summer and lived with her mother, while searching for a job in New York and lifeguarding at the pool in D.C. And in the first of her many political commitments to come, she worked on the democratic presidential campaign for Adlai Stevenson, Governor of Illinois, who ran unsuccessfully against Dwight D. Eisenhower; she had been instrumental in writing and printing a student newsletter about him. Gloria's life was full, but her heart was in turmoil.

Although her early life had been difficult, she began to see that there had been an advantage to having experienced such hardship—it had made her stronger. She remarked, "I might owe my own survival to the very East Toledo neighborhood I worked so hard to escape."[11] Her need to control her own life, to improve it, and to overcome obstacles in her own way also grew within her. This drive, this craving to succeed on her own, gave her a personal internal imperative, which was unique for her time, and incited life-changing results.

Her struggle to become Gloria soon outweighed her love for Blair and the societal mandate to get married. A few months before her graduation, the International Relations Organization's Asian Scholarship Fund offered two $1,000 Chester Bowles scholarships, named for the former American ambassador to India, to graduating Smith seniors for postgraduate study in that country. Bowles had declined his speaking fee from the previous year, and the money had been earmarked for the scholarship.

As Gloria had thought she was to marry when the scholarship was first offered, she did not bother to apply, although she had been very interested in the project. Later, when she met one of the recipients and learned that the second woman had backed out, Gloria wrote to the professor in charge to say that she was no longer engaged and that she had always had an interest in India. She had done a great deal of class work on the country with prime results and had been steeped in the culture as a child, due to Ruth's fervent leaning toward Theosophy. Although she had fibbed about her impending marriage, Gloria's scholarship was approved.

This completely negated the wedding. One early morning in New York, after spending the night with Blair, Gloria slipped out of the room and left the engagement ring on the nightstand with a note, telling him she could not go through with the marriage. Blair was crushed and wrote to her several times over the next few years, but she never answered his mail. Gloria was off for India.

NOTES

1. Quoted in Allison J. Petrozziello, "Gloria Steinem on Smith in the '50s," *NewsSmith*, 25 January 2000, http://www.smith.edu/newssmith/NSWint01/steinem.html.

2. John Palmer Gavit, "Smith College Teaches Girls to Be Self-Reliant," *New York Evening Post*, November–January 1992. *Five Colleges Digital Archives Project*, http://clio.fivecolleges.edu/smith/writings/1922gavit/1922series/13.gif.

3. Gloria Steinem, "Always Ask the Turtle," *Yuni Library*, http://www.yuni.com/library/docs/217.html.

4. Steinem, *Moving Beyond Words*, p. 122.

5. Quoted in Kate Moses, "The Real Sylvia Plath," *Salon*, 30 May 2000, http://dir.salon.com/books/feature/2000/05/30/plath1/index.html.

6. The current value would be more than $16,000.

7. Quoted in Stern, *Gloria Steinem*, p. 77.

8. Quoted in Heilbrun, *Education of a Woman*, p. 56.

9. Quoted in Stern, *Gloria Steinem*, p. 81.

10. Ibid., p. 87.

11. Steinem, *Outrageous* Acts, p. 144.

Chapter 5

LIFE IN INDIA

Although Gloria's Chester Bowles scholarship provided $1,000, the amount was not nearly enough to cover her expenses. It would cost $1,200 for the round-trip flight alone. Obviously, she needed to supplement the grant to survive.

Gloria contacted magazines, offering to write articles about her time in India, but had little success in securing assignments that would pay enough to matter. She ultimately made a deal with Trans World Airlines (TWA) to write publicity for the company in exchange for complimentary airfare. However, almost as soon as the agreement was made, TWA rescinded the offer, and Gloria was back to square one. She was so disappointed that a TWA employee took pity on her and agreed to finance the trip one way, if she would write a brochure about India.

She was so anxious to get away from Blair, from the allure of being in love, and from tying herself down to one man, that she took off for London in 1956 to await visa approval for India, which was actually still uncertain. She had to wait for days, then weeks, and finally, with her meager funds dwindling, she had to find a job—any job that would support her. Yet, she had no working papers in England. The best job she could secure without them was as a server in an espresso shop.

Gloria enjoyed the atmosphere at her job. Students from many different nations frequented the place and it was in a good neighborhood. Although anxious about her visa, she was comfortable—until she learned that she was pregnant.

A SERIOUS CONUNDRUM

In the 1950s, having a baby out of wedlock was a disaster for women. Single mothers were thought of as women of loose morals and treated with derision, along with their children. Unwed mothers had four choices in those days. One was to keep the baby, support it and herself, and hope that her illegitimate child would not suffer lasting emotional scars. However, without patronage of some type—from parents, the baby's father, or others—this solution was destined, in most cases, to ensure a life of poverty for the woman and her child. It was virtually impossible for women to secure high-paying jobs in the late 1950s, and having come from a life of dire poverty, this option was not at all attractive to Gloria; she certainly did not want that life for her child.

Her second option was to admit the circumstances to Blair and get married. Although Gloria was quite sure that Blair was the father of this baby, she did not want to consign herself and her child to life with an unfulfilled mother, just as her own mother had done. To Gloria, marriage seemed like prison, one that a woman could never escape. If she married and then things did not work out, divorce was also a difficult decision. Lawful divorce was not easily obtained, and the action was considered a personal failure at that time. After weighing these possibilities, Gloria decided that marriage was simply out of the question.

The third option was to carry the baby full term and then give it up for adoption when it was born. This continues to be a complex decision for women, involving the choice of proper adoptive parents, not to mention the traumatic effect of carrying a baby for nine months, seeing its face, and giving it away. Although women who choose this option see it as a way to give their children better lives, they still carry the heartache of losing their babies for the rest of their lives. Since Gloria had been mentally abandoned by her own mother, would she be repeating a pattern? Neither delivery nor adoption was an option for her.

Pregnancy would hamper her exploration of India. Also, Europe and Asia had different laws from those of the United States, and different customs. Would adoption even be an alternative in India, and how would the people treat her when she was pregnant without a husband? How would they treat her child?

The fourth option, abortion, is a most difficult choice for a woman to make, even when she believes the fetus in its early stages is not yet a human being. In the 1950s, the procedure was also illegal, without some conditions met. In London, where Gloria was staying, two doctors would have to certify that the mother would be mentally and physically injured by allowing the pregnancy to continue to full term. In lieu of that documentation, illegal abortions, often performed by spurious practitioners with little regard for hygiene, were not only distasteful and frightening, they were physically dangerous.

AN INDEPENDENT DECISION

Gloria was desperate and clearly interested in dealing with the matter independently. She told no one, and when she pulled herself together, she realized that the only option for her was abortion and she wanted to have it done legally. Her firm belief remains that a woman ultimately should have control of her own body.

Gloria consulted the first doctor, a general practitioner named John Sharpe, whose number she chose from the telephone book. Gloria told him that the father of her baby did not want to be married, not wanting to admit that she was the one who was not interested in being shackled by the contract for fear of the doctor's contempt. If he felt that she was selfishly making the decision to abort, she might not get the approval she needed. She did not mention abortion and hoped he would bring up the topic. Instead, he gave her a medication to bring on menstruation, but nothing happened. When she returned to Dr. Sharpe and asked about abortion, he agreed to sign the form and sent her to another doctor for the operation on the condition that she promised to do what she really wanted to do with her life.

Dr. Sharpe referred her to a woman doctor for the abortion, and she was not at all sympathetic to Gloria's predicament. In fact, she was contemptuous and said that Gloria had waited too long to terminate the pregnancy; it was nearly too late for the abortion. Yet, she agreed to participate only because Dr. Sharpe had recommended her.

If not understanding, the woman doctor was efficient. She performed the abortion competently and cleanly, and after a few days in bed, Gloria was relieved, although the abortion had cost her nearly $500, which was half her savings. But her financial standing was not important to her at that point. She had taken complete charge of her life and said, "[For] the first time I stopped passively accepting whatever happened to me and took responsibility."[1] In later years, this experience would become the catalyst that would allow her to embrace feminism and her strong pro-choice stand, which she prefers to call reproductive freedom.

On January 27, 1957, her visa finally came through from India. On her way to southern Asia, she stopped in Geneva to see a friend and then traveled on to Greece, where she visited the Acropolis.

She finally boarded a plane for India, the second most populous country in the world. On February 24, 1957, when she landed in Bombay (or Mumbai), the capital of the Indian state of Maharashtra and India's main port and commercial center, she immediately fell in love with the place. The archipelago of seven islands, which attracted throngs of both rich and poor, had people of all classes crowding the streets. Although India is as different from the United States as fire is to water, Gloria felt at home for the first time in her life. Breathing in the pungent, exotic smells of Indian spices, even mixed with the smell of cow dung from the holy cattle that were allowed to wander unfettered in the streets, Gloria was comfortable, although she was an outsider.

She spent a few days with the family of a TWA employee and then flew on to New Delhi, the capital of India. Here, she met another young woman named Jean Joyce, who had accompanied Chester Bowles to India and then, lost her job when the Eisenhower administration took over in the United States and replaced Bowles as India's ambassador. Jean loved India so much that she secured another position with the Ford Foundation and stayed. She was eager to offer Gloria a place to settle for a while.

BECOMING A NATIVE

Gloria accepted Jean's offer and soon got into the native politics and customs. She began to wear saris—unstitched yards of cloth wrapped around the waist to form a skirt with the free end draped over the shoulder or the head. Completing the outfit is a blouse that ends just under the bust and a petticoat under the sari's skirt. Since it had been only 10 years since India had achieved its independence from Great Britain, India was a very poor nation, and Gloria wanted to fit in rather than seem the rich American. She felt much more at home dressed as one of the Indian people, rather than wearing the Smith Bermuda shorts she had brought along on the trip. By reading the local press, she saw that India was aggressive in their efforts to improve food production via new farming methods, and was impressed by the government's ambition to correct problems and its compassion toward the poor.

Yet, India was still backward when it came to women. Soon Gloria and Kayla Achter, the second scholarship recipient, moved into Miranda

House at the University of New Delhi, which had a more liberal code of behavior for women. One of two women's colleges within the university structure, Miranda permitted women who lived there to leave the campus in smaller groups than the four generally required and had a curfew of 8:00 P.M., which was later than other dormitories. As American oddities in residence, the girls were quite popular.

Some of the Indian girls' questions concerned Western religion, rock and roll, and dating. However, political sentiment for the United States was at low ebb at this time. Many of the girls asked why America had supplied arms to Pakistan during the India-Pakistan War of 1947–49. Gloria and Kayla answered all the questions that they could and even performed American songs and dances for their Indian dorm mates, who in turn performed Indian songs and dances for them.

As constant targets of attention, Gloria and Kayla were also invited to a myriad of social functions and, through their attendance, learned many of the social customs of India, including how to eat with their hands, which involves actually putting one's hands into one's mouth, and how to properly wear a sari. Gloria found differences between American and Indian culture interesting. For instance, at that time in America, it was impolite for a woman to show off her midriff, while in India, it was not proper to show her legs. However, the girls had to learn many other cultural differences.

An important rule was never to use one's left hand when accepting gifts or when interacting with others. It is custom to clean oneself after going to the toilet with the left hand, which is considered to be unclean. Shoes and feet also have a tainted stigma. Shoes and feet must never touch another person, and shoes must always be kept on the floor and never worn inside a person's house; however, staring is perfectly acceptable as are personal questions about income, age, or cost. One antithetical gesture is moving one's head from side to side when meaning no, because in India, the gesture means yes.

Politically, the United States and India had even less in common. In 1957, India was in a state of political infancy. Mohandas Gandhi had successfully marshaled the Indian people in a nonviolent revolution, which led to the dissolution of British colonial rule and independence for the country only 10 years earlier. At that time, Pakistan was part of British colonial India and predominantly Muslim, while other parts of the country were overwhelmingly Hindu. When colonial India won independence, an agreement was made to partition the two territories, making each an independent nation—India and Pakistan.

Whereas colonial states were given the option of joining either of the two nations when the British relinquished control, the territories of Jammu and Kashmir remained uncommitted, until armed soldiers forced them to sign an Instrument of Accession to India. Pakistan never accepted the agreement, and so war broke out soon after the British left the area, with India and Pakistan still claiming important areas held by the other. The disagreement over this land continues to the present day.

THE TURMOIL OF INDIAN POLITICS

Jawaharlal Nehru was elected the prime minister of India in the first national election in 1947. As a follower of Gandhi, Nehru had participated in negotiations for a free and independent India with the British government and carried on Gandhi's legacy after his assassination in 1948. Nehru opposed the division of the colonial territory and held that all Indians should be equal citizens of the new nation, regardless of religion. Yet, division was the fastest route to independence, and Nehru reluctantly agreed to the partitioning.

As the Cold War developed, Nehru tried to keep India neutral. Yet, in 1950, the Chinese invaded Tibet, claiming its suzerain rights, which Tibet denied they had. This suzerainty meant that China assumed the role of protector over Tibet, while allowing the country autonomous control in domestic affairs. The Tibetans claimed that these rights were negated by the Thirteenth Dalai Lama's declaration of independence in 1911; however, the Chinese did not recognize this claim. Nehru tried to persuade the Fourteenth Dalai Lama, the spiritual and temporal ruler of Tibet, to cooperate with the Chinese; yet, his involvement in the issue raised conflict between India and China, and the tension between the countries continued to brew during Gloria's stay.

Politically, she was against the Communist party in India, which had sided with the British during the independence movement. She backed the Gandhi faction and made many lifelong friends through her association with the party. Gandhi's bequest to cause political change to help the poor through nonviolent activism was highly worthwhile to Gloria, as she always identified with the lower classes. However, the poverty existing in India nearly overwhelmed her. She remarked, "How will I ever, ever become accustomed to the bundle of dirty rags on the sidewalk which often as not turns out to be a little boy?"[2]

In May 1957, when the school term ended, Gloria boarded with an Indian family in New Delhi for 80 cents a day and continued to soak in the city and Indian culture. Through her explorations, she met the daughter of Prime Minister Nehru, Indira Gandhi,[3] when Mrs. Gandhi served as the official hostess at a youth gathering for her father. She and Gloria discussed several issues, including how Gloria could best spend her time in India.

For 10 days that month, Gloria visited a radical humanist study camp in the Himalayan foothills. These theorists are proponents of radical change, from an objective stance, with a goal of freeing man from the social structures in which they live. These philosophies would be extremely influential in Gloria's later years, and the experience would further change her philosophies on Marxism. She had been drawn to the Marxist perspective during the McCarthy era, as she felt that Marxism and McCarthyism were juxtaposed, which made Marxism attractive merely by its extreme difference. However, the Marxist stance asserts that the ends justify the means. With the radical humanists, Gloria learned that the ends are dictated by the means chosen, and that the Marxist philosophy was doomed to failure via moral degeneration.

FINANCIAL DIFFICULTIES

Back in the United States, Chester Bowles was concerned about what the women in India were learning. Smith had not set a distinct course of study for the two fellows, although they did have to file periodic reports. Bowles worried about the disorganization of Smith's plans. Soon it was learned that the Chester Bowles Scholarship Committee was $700 in debt, while the third woman was scheduled to leave for India in the fall of 1957. After this disclosure, the Committee chairperson conceded that they had been idealistic in their expectations and suspended the program until they could repay the $700 owed to the student bank at Smith. However, the program never resumed. The two women in India were the only recipients to ever receive the Chester Bowles scholarship.

Gloria's own money problems continued to plague her. TWA paid her by check for the brochure she had written about India; however, she had no bank account and no means of cashing it. When she wrote home, she constantly asked for money and advised her family to wash any new clothes they might send to her, as there was an Indian tax on new clothing coming into the country and she did not have the funds to afford the tariff. Yet, little money was readily available at home to send; so, Gloria did odd jobs. She assisted in designing sandals and writing promotional material for them, posed for a few ads, and wrote *The Thousand Indias,* a guidebook for the Indian government, encouraging American students and teachers to visit the county. She also had several freelance articles published in the Indian press.

At 23, Gloria was not only flying solo financially, she traveled alone as well. The camaraderie between the two American girls in India never solidified. Gloria found Kayla to be irresponsible and diametrically opposed to her own state of mind. They went separate ways when the semester ended, and after Gloria's visit to the radical humanists, where she learned that radical didn't have to connote violence or lunacy, but "going to the root,"[4] she visited the home of Theosophy in Madras. To get there, she bought a third-class railway ticket and discovered that women were still watched over in India. To evade male attentions, women were given a separate car in which to travel. Men were not allowed to touch women in public, not even to shake hands. In contrast, married women were considered to be possessions of their husbands and many were beaten when they did not obey their spouses or locked in rooms without food for days.

Learning about these customs was upsetting for Gloria, but traveling with Indian women was interesting in other ways and Gloria interested her traveling companions as well. She felt as if she was getting into the real India as she moved farther south. The women were astonished that Gloria was unmarried and without children and asked her how she accomplished such a feat. Women in India were married early, often by arrangement, and poor women had little or no access to birth control. Even when they found a viable method, they had to hide it from their husbands, who forbade any such devices.

Gloria traveled as far as Kerala, near the southern tip of India. Here, a new Indian (rather than Soviet) Communist government had recently taken over, and she sought to assess its effectiveness; she interviewed 10 different plantation owners there. She also journeyed to an ashram, a religious community, run by a follower of Gandhi, Vinoba Bhave, who had begun the Bhoodan, or land gift movement, in 1951. In Gandhi fashion, the goal of the Bhoodan was for proponents to travel from village to village on foot asking property-owners to contribute land to the poor, who often worked the land without ownership. Although the movement had begun to wane in 1957, the walking parties had taken on the onus of quelling riots that had broken out in the countryside.

As Gloria arrived at the ashram, new groups were forming. She met a Protestant missionary from the United States who wanted her to travel with his group. He convinced her that she was no more unusual to the people of southern India than other Indians from the north, west, and east, as Indians are as diverse in cultures and languages as the different peoples of Europe. Gloria's mixture of English and Hindi, the most widely spoken language in India, was certainly no more unusual than the language of an Indian person from another region, who would speak another of the 14 major languages in that country.

Another reason for persuading her to go was that men were not able to go into Hindu women's quarters. They needed Gloria to visit women and demonstrate that they were welcome to join in the discussions. Gloria jumped at the chance to involve other women in the events shaping the world around them. She wanted to help them improve their status, and later wrote, "Girls are much less likely to be sent to school that the national female literacy rate is less than half that for males...and their humanity is so minimally acknowledged that killing a wife in order to take another wife—and get another dowry—is one of the major sufferings addressed by the women's movement."[5]

WALKING FOR PEACE

Once she accepted the mission, Gloria became a link in a chain of peacemakers, who followed the tradition of the Hindu holy aesthetics, known as sadhus, and carried only begging cups, combs, and the clothes they wore, which was symbolic of the sadhus' trust in God. This group had faith in people who wanted peace and trusted them to offer food and lodging.

As the group went from village to village, they held meetings in the cool early morning, walked and slept during the heat of the day, and met people at night by the light of kerosene lanterns.

It seemed to Gloria that discontents wanted merely to vent their frustrations over the inequities of the caste system, a social hierarchy that designates a person's class at birth. Dates of the system's origin vary widely, between 1500 B.C. to 500 B.C., depending on the event leading up to the separation of classes. Most often, the caste system is based upon the date when Aryan races came to India. However, sociologist Oliver Cromwell Cox wrote, "In the first place, we do not know when the Aryans entered India; hence it may be futile to embark upon a discussion, the validity of which can depend only on definite knowledge of the date of Aryan immigration."[6]

Clearly, however, this social hierarchy is based in Hindu mythology, which holds that all men were originally created Brahmans, who are the white or those who carry the attribute of goodness and are the priests and teachers. Through men's actions, lower castes were born. The Kshatriyas are the red Brahmans who possessed the attribute of passion. These are the warriors and rulers. The yellow Vaisyas held both goodness and passion and became the traders, cattlemen, farmers, and artisans. The black Sudras were those Brahmans who fell away from purity of behavior and succumbed to the element of darkness. They were charged with menial labor. These four groups are known as the basic Varna, which does not mean class or status, but skin color.

Among these Varnas are 3,000 castes and 25,000 subcultures, called Jats, so that even Brahmans look down upon other Brahmans of a lower Jat. This caste system dictates not only occupation but also dietary regimen and sets guidelines by which castes may interact with one another.

The Sudras are not considered the lowest class of people in India however. The lowest class of people are said to be without caste and are called the Dalits, the broken people or the untouchables. Dalits are treated as no more than slaves and are reduced to cleaning human feces and dead animals from the streets with their hands. They may not use the same wells as members of higher castes and their children are forced to sit in the back of classrooms. They live in extreme poverty and have no prospects for the future. Hindus believe that the untouchables are repaying a debt of karma (cause and effect) from a previous life.

Mohandas Gandhi tried to break this cycle of oppression when he called for Dalit liberation. Caste discrimination had even been made illegal in 1950, as the newly liberated India was determined to move into a democratic society where everyone was equal. However, the caste system still existed in rural areas of India in 1956 as it does today. With such a complex hierarchy, the castes were bound to have confrontations, and disputes often arose over land or inequity.

Gloria's role in these meetings was mainly to sit and listen to people's complaints. Many times after a discussion, group leaders would avow to settle disputes amicably, and she learned from this what optimism and resolve could accomplish.

During her daily walk, Gloria would often bathe in streams to cool herself, fully clothed, and allow her sari to dry as she walked, just as the other members of her party did. At night, village people fed the group rice cakes and sweet milky tea and shared their sleeping mats. Eventually, the violence quelled.

PHYSICAL LIMITATIONS

Gloria's tender feet were severely blistered by the continual walking. Infection set in and she found it necessary to hitch a ride on an oxcart, back to the bus and then to the ashram. The Bhoodan marches continued from 1951 to 1964 and yielded more than four million acres of land for the poor. Prime Minister Nehru told parliament, "This frail man [Vinoba Bhave] has just accomplished, solely by the force of nonviolence, what all the military power of the Government would be unable to do [through forced collectivization.]"[7] Gloria came away seeing how grass roots meetings could affect change.

When Gloria's feet healed, she moved to a YWCA in Bombay and enjoyed the city until her money was gone and then borrowed more money to stay longer, as she could live quite well on 50 cents a day. She also sought ways to make it back to the United States, and after 18 months in India, she finally had enough money to go home. Of her time in India, she wrote, "Most of us have a few events that divide our lives into 'before' and 'after.' This was one for me."[8]

But the trip was not over. She took the train to Rangoon, Burma, with a stop in Calcutta (or Kolkata) for a time, long enough to audit classes at Calcutta University. She was also persuaded to have her horoscope cast. She was surprised when the astrologer told her she had lived in the Indian state of Bengal (of which Calcutta is the capital) in another life, but that she must have done something terrible to have been reborn in the United States.

When she finally arrived in Rangoon, she checked into a hotel there and woke up to find that a coup had taken place overnight, but it had been peaceful and she was not affected.

After a long flight, she found herself in Hong Kong, staying at the YWCA again. She also visited Tokyo and Kyoto, and by July 1958, it was time for her to leave Asia. She sailed steerage class on the *President Cleveland*, where the crew would sneak her above boards to mingle with the privileged passengers.

When Gloria docked in San Francisco, Leo met her. She learned immediately that he was too broke to get her back to Washington, D.C., so they worked their way across country, buying and selling antiques and antique jewelry. On their route, they made a stop in Las Vegas, where Leo was sure Gloria would win a jackpot.

When they finally got back to D.C., Gloria was full of enthusiasm for the months she had spent in Asia and was bursting to tell anyone who would listen about her adventures. However, no one seemed interested. Once again, she felt like a nobody and quickly set her sights on the lights in New York City.

NOTES

1. Quoted in Heilbrun, *Education of a Woman*, p. 69.

2. Quoted in Stern, *Gloria Steinem*, p. 101.

3. Indira Gandhi would be prime minister of India in the years 1966–77 and 1980–84. She was assassinated by two of her own bodyguards in 1984 in response to an attack ordered on a Sikh shrine, the Golden Temple, in June of that year.

4. Steinem, *Moving Beyond Words*, p. 264.

5. Steinem, *Revolution from Within*, p. 54.

6. Cox and Roucek, *Caste, Class, and Race*, p. 92.

7. Quoted in Patrick Iber, "Bhoodan and Gramdan," *Spiritual Socialism, Gentle Anarchism, and Sarvodaya—The Welfare of All,* http://www.stanford.edu/~piber/nonviolence/history/bhoodan_and_gramdan.html.

8. Steinem, *Moving Beyond Words*, p. 266.

Chapter 6

FREELANCING IN
NEW YORK CITY

When Gloria returned to the United States from India in 1958, she first went to Washington, D.C., to visit her family, and then continued on to New York City to look for suitable work. She was filled with compassion for the underclasses, after seeing the poverty in India and man's inhumanity to man, and insisted that she sit in the front seat with New York cab drivers, so as not to make them feel subservient. While in India, she had ridden in several rickshaws, and found the idea of portage under the power of another human being distasteful. However, New York cab drivers were less than enthusiastic about Gloria's good intentions.

Much had changed in the United States in the two years since she had left the country. Americans were spending more than ever before and, in the economic balance, got more for less money. Hot items were new household appliances—electric can openers, dishwashers, refrigerators with bigger freezers than previous models, and new TVs. Popular music had taken a different tack. Elvis was the king of rock and roll and in 1956 made his famed first appearance on the revered *Ed Sullivan Show*. At the movies, James Dean and Marilyn Monroe caused throbbing hearts, and General Dwight D. Eisenhower was president.

When Gloria first arrived in the city of New York, the Solomon R. Guggenheim Museum, designed by architect Frank Lloyd Wright, was in its last stages of completion. Nelson Rockefeller would become governor that year, and Mickey Mantle, Yogi Berra, and Whitey Ford would help the New York Yankees win the World Series, beating the Milwaukee Braves four games to three.

The city was alive with young Ivy League and Seven Sisters graduates wanting to get into the publishing business. Finding a job would not be easy for Gloria, especially since she had set her sights on working at prestigious magazines such as the *Saturday Review*. As a new writer, her chances for succeeding would be low, especially since she was a woman.

The idea of women's equality had not surfaced in 1958 and would not even be considered for several years to come. Women were thought of as secretaries, researchers, librarians, teachers, and especially mothers, but they were definitely not thought much of as writers. The fact did not daunt Gloria's enthusiasm for the work. She was determined to succeed in a male-dominated world.

However, after meeting such luminaries as Chester Bowles and Indira Gandhi and nearly marrying the nephew of Jascha Heifetz, Gloria was determined to find higher ground than the local New York free rag, where most new writers got their start. Her writing resume included the brochure for TWA, *The Thousand Indias*, and various freelance works at Smith and in India, but her clips were not substantial enough to impress publishers of national magazines. To find the types of jobs she wanted, Gloria needed more experience.

In lieu of glamorous writing, she wanted to work with the underprivileged as she had done in India. Her first application was to the India Committee of the Asia Society, in hope that they might have public relations work in the field of writing. She also managed to acquire several interviews with the *Saturday Review*, but they finally turned her down, advising her that she would not be happy with the job they were offering. The quandary was that as a woman, she could not be hired for key positions and because she had a college degree, she was considered to be overqualified for others.

ON HER OWN

While trying to find the path to her aims, she moved into an apartment with a group of young women on West 57th Street, which runs along the western edge of Central Park to the Hudson River. Gloria was uncertain how her roommates supported themselves, as they had no jobs and went out every night; however, one of them had posed for a nude portrait, which hung on one wall of the apartment. A pay phone hung on another wall. She wondered how they got their money and began to realize that New York City would be a tough place to crack for any young, single woman, even herself.

A relationship she made in India finally helped her to start her New York career. Clive Gray, who was a former vice president of the National

Student Association (NSA), had met Gloria in India and was impressed with her knowledge of that country and of Indian students. When compiling a list of candidates who might work well on a new project involving a youth festival in Vienna, which was to take place in the summer of 1959, Gray remembered her.

More than 200 colleges and universities had student members of the NSA at the time. The organization was an offshoot of the International Union of Students (IUS), which had held its first world conference in Prague, Czechoslovakia, in 1946. That year, independent students had paid their own way to attend, hoping to meet minds with other young people around the world and affect change, especially on the cold war. Yet, conference attendees were shocked to see how Soviet students were able to manipulate the proceedings to disseminate the Communist viewpoint and decided they wanted a stronger organization to promote democratic interests in future world conferences. By 1947, the NSA was formed.

At its annual national conference, NSA students took a stand on American issues, such as lowering the voting age from 21 to 18 years. The NSA also lobbied on other issues, such as desegregation, in Washington. They also looked toward affecting the international picture at IUS proceedings. Suspicion had become proof that the IUS was Soviet controlled, when one of its officers became chief of the KGB, the Soviet secret police, in 1958.

At this point, the international organizations began competing for members from other nations, especially those emerging from third world countries. Because the IUS was run and supported by communists, it was more organized and businesslike than the NSA, which was funded solely through members' dues. Then, the Central Intelligence Agency (CIA), seeing an opportunity to win the minds of young communists, became involved and by 1951 was providing financial backing for NSA overseas activities. A 1991 *Campus Watch* article states: "[A]ccording to a *New York Times* interview with Frederic Delano Hoghteling, then NSA secretary, the CIA gave him several thousand dollars to pay traveling expenses for a delegation of twelve representatives to a European international student conference."[1]

A FIRST JOB IN PUBLIC RELATIONS

Clive Gray promoted Gloria's international expertise for the World Festival of Youth and Students for Peace and Friendship, to be held in Vienna and promoted jointly by the World Federation of Democratic Youth (WFDY), founded in London in 1945 by members from student groups from 63 countries, and the IUS. Participation was open to other students and student organizations around the world; however, the NSA was officially boycotting the proceedings in protest of participating in an overtly Soviet propaganda exercise. However, the NSA did encourage individual members to attend. The U.S. State Department gave this policy a green light.

One important reason for State Department approval was that historically the festivals had been sited in communist block countries. But in 1959, the conference was to be held in the democratic country of Austria. Communist delegates would be exposed not only to other noncommunist delegates, but also to a democratic place where people were free to speak their minds. "[This time, the State Department's] policy did not create unnecessary obstacles to participation by American youths who, as private individuals, felt that they could both learn and perhaps teach by observing the spectacle, the first of its kind to be held in a noncommunist country, and by seeking to break through communist stereotypes to real person-to-person communication with representatives of the communist youth movements sent out beyond the Iron Curtain to spread the Marxist-Leninist gospel."[2]

Gloria had wanted to attend the festival in 1957, which was held in Moscow. Yet, the Indian government made it difficult for students to attend, and she missed the opportunity to go. When a second opportunity to participate came up, she was quite willing to discuss working with ex-NSA international vice president Clive Gray to recruit and brief students to discuss the United States and democracy with communist students in informal seminars, thereby combating Soviet propaganda.

Gloria considered the work to be worthwhile, so she first met with Harry Lunn, ex-president of the NSA, who said he worked for the Defense Department but who was actually working for the CIA. Lunn approved Gloria and she was sent to Cambridge, Massachusetts, where she had several more interviews with various ex-NSA personnel. Paul Sigmund, another ex-NSA international vice president, would run the festival organization and he liked Gloria, as did the other men to interview her. She was offered the job of coexecutive director of the Independent Service for Information on the Vienna Youth Festival (ISI). Her primary responsibility would be public relations—getting press coverage for the festival, handling the media, and writing various publications.

Yet, Gloria had reservations. Senator Joseph McCarthy had just been censured by the Senate for his interrogations of alleged communists. Although the era of McCarthyism had ended, merely attending a communist sponsored conference might still cast a shadow on students wishing to go. Anticommunist sentiment was still high in America. Gloria also suspected that attendees would be investigated by the FBI, and that attendance at the conference might even be enough to prevent attendees from ever holding a government job.

Gloria was also concerned about the funding, and remarked, "Students were not taken seriously here before the civil rights movement, and private money receded at the mention of a Communist youth festival."[3] How would a new organization be able to pay to send students abroad? She was told that the conference would be funded through various means and that money was not an issue. CIA involvement was a two-sided coin.

STATE OF THE NATION

Right around the same time that Gloria became involved with the ISI, the CIA was going through a period of disgrace. Organized in 1947 for assemblage of foreign strategic intelligence and counterintelligence and participation in underground political activity, the CIA also distributes propaganda and false information in foreign countries where it wants to assert American influence. It soon became evident that their tactics were not always as they seemed.

Along with other leaders of free world countries, American President Dwight D. Eisenhower was concerned with the spread of Communism. In a 1955 letter to British Prime Minister Winston Churchill, he wrote: "We believe that if international Communism should penetrate the island barrier in the Western Pacific and thus be in a position to threaten the Philippines and Indonesia immediately and directly, all of us, including the free countries of Europe, would soon be in far worse trouble than we are now. Certainly that whole region would soon go."[4]

As the cold war intensified over the next few years, Indonesia accused the United States of intervening in the politics of their country and funding an army of rebels when a civil war broke out, while U.S. officials were busy denying involvement and claiming neutrality. However, it was proven that the CIA was indeed covertly funding Indonesian rebels to overthrow the regime of President Achmed Sukarno (or Soekarno) when a B-52 bomber, carrying pilot Allan Pope, was shot down on May 18. Pope was captured bearing documents to prove he was working for the CIA, and the incident was clear evidence that the intelligence community would use any means to stop the spread of communism.

At the time, America's ethical and moral standards were quite high. Any hint of wrongdoing was seen as subversive to the American value system by most U.S. citizens. When these events came to light, many Americans, especially young people, realized that even the president had lied to them, and the intelligence community's tactics were viewed as underhanded and dirty. To intensify their unease with the CIA, which was becoming highly active by the end of the 1950s, it soon became apparent that the agency was using the hallowed halls of many college campuses, especially Ivy League schools, to recruit educators and especially foreign language students into its ranks.

But Gloria did not see ISI as another operation of the CIA. She saw the organization as a front for the NSA, under CIA influence, and the ISI as independently controlled, and said, "I was never asked to report on other Americans or assess foreign nationals I had met."[5] She agreed to take the position.

Most of her work was done in Cambridge, although she was unhappy there. Her basement apartment took her back to Toledo days and because she knew only the men she worked with, she was lonely. Although she was at Harvard, an intellectual haven, she was an outsider and not completely happy with the job. It was not the type of writing she had intended to do, but she threw herself into the task and excelled at the position.

She wrote to her Aunt Janey, "It's a realization that, pretty often, the men who run Everything [sic] are just guys with gravy on their vests and not too much between the ears.... "[6]

COURTING IMPORTANT SOURCES

Gloria was the person who got CBS television network to agree to make a documentary of the Vienna conference. Yet, within three weeks of the conference's start, CBS cancelled the project, claiming it was not newsworthy. So, she went to New York City to see C. D. (Charles Douglas) Jackson, who was very powerful in media, as publisher of *Fortune* magazine. He was also the president of the Free Europe Committee, the parent of Radio Free Europe and Radio Liberty, which broadcasted uncensored information to boost democratic progress in countries behind the Iron Curtain.[7] Jackson had also written speeches for President Eisenhower and served as chief of psychological warfare during World War II and through much of Eisenhower's administration. Jackson had helped Gloria many times before, and at the time she approached him about the CBS with-drawal, he was an executive with Time-Life.

Jackson agreed to write to Frank Stanton, the president of CBS, and explain that he wanted to clear some ISI problems. He defended the youth festival as an important event in the cold war. As a result, Stanton invited Gloria to see him and insisted that they would not prepare an hour-long program, but agreed to supply a cameraman and a top corre-spondent, hoping to create a half-hour show.

During the last week of July, tens of thousands of young delegates flocked to the festival, bearing all the excitement and anticipation that young, spirited students with intentions of promoting world peace could have. On the other side of American delegates' amiable idealism was the intention to party. The Russians, however, were serious and under severe penalties from Russian authorities for not promoting the advantages of the communist point of view. Aside from the ubiquitous discussion groups and workshops, attendees found ballet, opera, and fireworks. Some of these delegates would later become well known to Americans, such as the future National Security Advisor to President Jimmy Carter, Zbigniew Brzezinski; author and social activist, Michael Harrington; and renowned *Washington Post* reporter, Walter Pincus.

As media representatives were not welcome within the festival, Gloria ran the press bureau from inside. She wrote press releases and offered del-egates for reporters to interview. Radio Free Europe strategist Sam Walker wrote to C. D. Jackson of her involvement: "Gloria is all you said she was, and then some."[8] She led an effective Independent Information Center and an International News Bureau, which published a daily festival news-paper in five different languages. Communists did everything they could to prevent distribution of such literature, even going so far as to assault de-livery personnel. Still, by the end of the conference, delegates and orga-nizers felt as if they had done a good job of swaying some young communists into a democratic direction.

When Gloria arrived back in Cambridge, she had one last job for the ISI—to prepare a report of the festival for publication, cowritten with Paul Sigmund, and she could not wait to get back to New York City. However, being in Cambridge was fortuitous in one important way. Walter Frieden-berg, with whom an intimate relationship had formed in India and whom she had even contemplated marrying, came to visit her in Cambridge.

He introduced her to his friend, Harold Hayes, an editor for *Esquire* magazine, and his wife Susan. Through Hayes, she met the then assistant art director of *Esquire*, Robert Benton, who would later find fame in Hollywood as the cowriter of *Bonnie and Clyde* and director of *Kramer vs. Kramer*.

A REAL THAT GIRL

When Gloria returned to New York in 1960, she found an apartment for $150 a month in a brownstone, across West 81st Street from the Museum of Natural History, which now also holds the Rose Center for Earth and Space and the Hayden Planetarium. Gloria's apartment had high windows, for which Ruth even came to New York City to sew curtains. Gloria mostly decorated with secondhand shop items and furnishings, including two huge reproductions of medieval-style chairs and a teacart that she painted red to resemble a little red wagon, which she had always wanted as a child. Yet, most of her belongings remained in boxes, as they would continue to do throughout most of her life. Gloria never seemed to find time to unpack, so she lived out of those boxes and suitcases for years.

To pay for her new independent life, Gloria needed a steady source of income, which she was not sure freelancing would provide. Professionally and personally, Susan Hayes came to be an important contact. Through her, she also met cartoonist Harvey Kurtzman, the creator of *Mad Magazine*. Kurtzman hired Gloria to be his assistant. He wanted to start a new humor magazine *(Help! For Tired Minds)*, and though she was paid for only part-time work, the position turned into a full-time job. She was responsible for setting up photo shoots, writing humorous captions, and persuading comedians, such as Dick Van Dyke, Milton Berle, and Sid Caesar, to appear on the cover. Terry Gilliam, well known for his direction of the Monty Python movies, *12 Monkeys*, and *Brazil*, was also a Kurtzman employee and became his assistant when Gloria left the position. Of her he said, "She sort of hid this part of her career, which is a great pity because she was brilliant."[9]

Her personal life was also gaining, as she began to frequent *Esquire* to help on projects, especially those involving Robert Benton. The atmosphere at the magazine was charged with the excitement of a high-profile publication. As a vanguard of New Journalism,[10] the magazine featured articles by Tom Wolfe, who would later write *Bonfire of the Vanities* and *A Man in Full*; Norman Mailer, author of *The Naked and the Dead* and the National Book Award and Pulitzer prizewinning *Armies of the Night*; and Gay Talese, who would come to write the best-selling story of mob boss

Joseph Bonanno in *Honor Thy Father*. Benton, along with David Newman, who was the fiction editor's assistant at that time and with whom Benton would write several screenplays including *Bonnie and Clyde* and *Superman*, had begun to produce innovative, quick pieces with lots of graphics and tongue-in-cheek social commentary. They and a few others decided the cool content for the magazine.

Gloria wrote a few small pieces for *Esquire* that were not credited. Her first byline came in July 1961 for her piece "Sophisticated Fun & Games." She also wrote captions for fashion spreads and recipes for bachelors.

Benton and Gloria's close association soon led to dating, and Gloria admits it was the first time she fell in love, declaring that Blair Chotzinoff had been a heavy infatuation. She had not shared interests with Chotzinoff as she did with Benton. Gloria and Robert were the same age and really connected.

The couple spent a great deal of time with future graphic design director and president of *New York* magazine, Milton Glaser, and his wife, Shirley. When Henry Wolf joined the foursome, with whatever date he happened to be courting at the time, Gloria made another important contact—Barbara Nessim.

NEW FRIENDS

In 1961, Gloria's landlord raised her rent and she fretted over what to do because she was unable to afford the increase. She was happy to meet Barbara and soon asked her to become her roommate. Rather than accept the rent increase, they looked for another apartment, and found only a small studio to share on East 71st Street. Several months later, however, Gloria was lucky to find a larger studio apartment for $125 a month on a commercial block filled with restaurants and offices. The new apartment was above Steak Pommes Frites, a French café, and had a square bathtub and two beds, which were community property. Whoever fell asleep first, took the corner bed. For warmth and ambience, there was a brick fireplace; and Gloria's desk was in one corner of the room, and Barbara's art supplies in another.

The two women were dissimilar in many ways. Barbara was six years younger than Gloria, and had no interest whatsoever in politics. She was on her way to becoming a commercial artist[11] because she saw it as a path to a steady income, as well as thinking that fine artists were too depressed. She was most interested with being able to support herself through her work. Gloria was tall and willowy with a Smith education, a quick wit, and a quiet reserve; Barbara was talkative, lively, and came from the Bronx, sporting a thick Bronx accent.

Yet, the women were similar in ways that count. They were equally generous, were not hell-bent on marriage, and were eager to pursue their careers to achieve success. They spent a great deal of time together working in the apartment and never argued. Nessim said, "We each knew we had a place in this world."[12]

Gloria's relationship with Benton was another good match. They enjoyed free movie screenings because of complimentary tickets provided to *Esquire*. They usually liked not only the same movies, but also the same books. However, unlike Gloria, Benton was not the least bit interested in politics.

One of the best parts of the relationship was that both were writers and encouraged each other. She also felt close enough to him to tell him about the misery she had suffered in Toledo, when he said to her, "Tell me a Toledo story."[13] He helped her to see that she could be herself and that her background did not matter. All that was important was who Gloria had become and what she was doing at the present time.

Along with folks from the magazine, Benton and Gloria socialized with other writers like Liz Smith, Harvey Schmidt, and Tom Jones, known lovingly in New York City as the Texas Mafia. While Smith would go on to become the *New York Post* gossip columnist, Schmidt and Jones would write and produce *The Fantasticks*, the longest running musical in the world, among other Broadway delights such as *I Do! I Do!* and *The Four Poster*. Gloria enjoyed being with the group, as they felt as much like outsiders as she did herself.

A MAJOR TRAGEDY AND A FIRST BREAK

Things were going rather well for Gloria, until April 20, 1961, when she received a phone call that her father had been in a car accident and was near death in an Orange County, California, hospital. Gloria immediately set off to go to him, but he died before she arrived. Sue had her paged at a layover in a Chicago airport to explain what had happened, but Gloria continued on to California. Leo's body was cremated and his ashes sent back to Washington, D.C., where a memorial service was held.

Gloria loved her father very much, free spirit that he was. She believed that he gave her strength, not fear, and enthusiasm for the unknown. She had spent her early childhood living on the edge with her parents; so the idea that she was alone, living on her own in the city of New York with a freelance income, and not knowing when or where the money would come from next seemed normal to her. This strength to live in chaos was her inheritance from Leo, a bestowal that would carry her through for most of her life.

Gloria stayed a few days in California to sort through her father's belongings, and since he traveled constantly, most of the things he owned were in his car. Some of the objects were his; some belonged to others. One interesting item was a ring bearing an inscription to boxer Rocky Marciano and a three-carat diamond. Gloria called Marciano and told him about the find. He came to pick up the ring, took it away to have it appraised, and never contacted her again. She flippantly uses the story to show her lack of business acumen.

Back in New York City, still grieving for her father, the number of Gloria's writing assignments grew to take her mind away from sorrow. She also learned of another youth festival, which was to be held in Helsinki, Finland. The ISI contacted her, though in 1959 the organization had changed its name to Independent Research Service (IRS), to assume her former position. As she was too busy fulfilling writing assignments, she agreed to help in whatever way she could, but strictly on a volunteer basis when she was available, although she agreed to help with the festival's press conference. To help her with the public relations, she enlisted the help of many friends and acquaintances including Clay Felker, the features editor at *Esquire Magazine,* and Sam Antupit, the art director for *Show Magazine,* another of her sources for writing assignments. They would publish the festival newspaper in English, French, and Spanish and were told that the festival was being financed by Danish businessmen who did not want Helsinki to be Soviet controlled.

Once at the festival, Clay Felker became impressed with Gloria's organizational skills and her political astuteness. Felker's awareness of her would lead him to become most influential to her writing career, although he had the intuition about her proficiency long before the festival began. "My first break came when Clay Felker, then an editor at *Esquire,* assigned me an article on the newly developed contraceptive pill. It was my first signed article and helped me get other assignments. However, they were rarely plums, since those tended to be assigned to male writers."[14]

Before the Pill was developed, women were virtually victims of their biology. Although other forms of birth control were available, none were so effective in preventing unwanted pregnancy as the Pill. Taken on a regular schedule, it had been proven to be 99 percent effective in controlling a woman's fertility cycle and it was almost immediately accepted by a large segment of the feminine population. Author David Halberstam wrote, "In May 1960, the FDA approved Enovid as a contraceptive device. By the end of 1961 some 408,000 American women were taking the Pill...."[15]

Gloria finally had her first serious assignment and amassed piles of research. She labored seriously to turn it into an informative yet witty piece. When Felker saw it, he told her that it needed work and joked that she had actually managed to make sex seem dull. He helped her to rewrite the article until it was publishable as "The Moral Disarmament of Betty Coed" and it appeared in *Esquire*'s September 1962 issue. She wrote about the prevailing attitudes regarding sex. The Pill eliminated one deterring factor—the fear of pregnancy and thereby began a major shift in society. Gloria wrote, "Constant fear was hardly the case prior to the Pill in this country, but removing the last remnants of fear of social consequences seems sure to speed American women, especially single women, toward the view that their sex practices are none of society's business."[16]

NOTES

1. Phil Agee Jr., "CIA Infiltration of Student Groups: The National Student Association Scandal," *Campus Watch*, fall 1991, pp. 12–13.

2. Barghoorn, *Soviet Cultural Offensive*, p. 25.

3. "CIA Subsidized Student Trips," *New York Times*, 21 February 1967, p. 33.

4. Boyle, *The Churchill-Eisenhower Correspondence*, p. 190.

5. "CIA Subsidized Student Trips," p. 33.

6. Quoted in Heilbrun, *Education of a Woman*, p. 89.

7. A military and psychological block between countries of the free world and communist countries of the Soviet Block. In 1946, England's prime minister, Winston Churchill, coined the phrase in a speech at Westminster College in Missouri.

8. Quoted in Stern, *Gloria Steinem*, pp. 120–21.

9. Paul Wardle, "Terry Gilliam," excerpted from *The Comics Journal*, no. 182, http://www.tcj.com/2_archives/i_gilliam.html.

10. New Journalism took nonfiction to a different level by taking strict factual reportage and molding it through the use of fictional tools, such as sensory details and narrative analysis, in order to convey topics in a more flowing, readable style.

11. She would, however, be an acclaimed international modern artist with works in the permanent collection of the Smithsonian Institution and the Museum of Modern Art in Sweden, among other prestigious places.

12. Cohen, *The Sisterhood*, p. 113.

13. Quoted in Heilbrun, *Education of a Woman*, p. 93.

14. Steinem, interview, 2 February 2003.

15. David Halberstam, *The Fifties* (New York: Villard Books, 1993), p. 605.

16. Gloria Steinem, "The Moral Disarmament of Betty Coed," *Esquire*, September 1962, p. 155.

Gloria, in front of her Clark Lake, Michigan, home, 1945. Courtesy of Gloria Steinem.

Gloria with accordion, 6th grade, Toledo, Ohio. Photographer unknown. Courtesy of Smith College Archives, Smith College.

Gloria wearing a Sari. Courtesy of Gloria Steinem

Gloria Steinem and Dorothy Pitman Hughes, 1968. Photo by Dan Wynn. Courtesy of Smith College Archives, Smith College.

Gloria Steinem, in center, talking to a group of women, n.d. Photographer unknown. Gloria Steinem Papers. Courtesy of Smith College Archives, Smith College.

Gloria Steinem, n.d. Photographer unknown. Gloria Steinem Papers. Courtesy of Smith College Archives, Smith College.

Chapter 7

THE WRITING LIFE

In 1962, at about the same time that "Betty Coed" hit the newsstands, Gloria wrote an article for *Show* magazine, declaring the Helsinki festival a dismal failure. Yet, Gloria was able to provide one good slap to annoy the communist organizers of the conference.

Near the festival's end, the Soviets had tested their largest nuclear device, and she saw their actions as ripe with potential. She had signs reading, "Stop the Bomb" and "No Testing, East or West" made up and sent marchers to carry the placards past a ship where East German delegates were housed. When a Soviet festival organizer saw the signs, he became so angry that he seized one of them and tore it to shreds. Depending on just such an eventuality, Gloria had a photographer stationed and ready for the photo opportunity. The resultant snapshot was publicized throughout the world press and highly embarrassed the Soviets to everyone's delight.

In New York City that same year, Gloria and Robert Benton began skirting the idea of marriage, but the concept was still distasteful to Gloria. She and Benton were very much in love, and had a professional bond through writing. They both admit that each helped the other to have confidence in their ability to write and to continue writing. They equally ascribe transformation of their lives to the relationship. But to Gloria, marriage still had the potential to overshadow her individuality.

In 1963, Gloria ultimately decided that she was not getting married—to anyone—and her decision was the end of her relationship with Benton, although they parted amicably and still remain friends. It had been a year-and-a-half-long attachment, and though she felt she probably would marry someday, she just was not ready to make the compromise.

A FIRST BOOK

When Gloria and Benton parted ways, they still had a joint project to complete, as they had signed a contract with Viking Press to write an anthology entitled *The Pleasure Book*. In it, they had planned to use stock photographs, illustrations, and writing along with new clever pieces in the style of *Esquire* or *Show*. However, after their rift, Benton suggested she finish the book with Sam Antupit, and the publisher agreed. They also agreed to change the title to *The Beach Book*, which was published in 1963 and included a recount of the shipwreck that Gloria's great-grandfather survived in 1854:

> TERRIBLE SHIPWRECK AND LOSS OF LIFE
> WRECK OF THE SHIP *NEW ERA* OF BREMEN
> 75 BODIES WASHED ASHORE NEAR LONG BRANCH
> PROBABLY LOSS OF THREE HUNDRED LIVES
> Long Beach, New Jersey. Mon., November 13, 1 P.M. The ship *New Era* of Bath Maine from Bremen, bound to New York with about 300 passengers on board consigned to C.C. Duncan, went ashore last night in dense fog off Deal on the Jersey coast and will probably be a total wreck.
> SECOND DISPATCH: The ship *New Era* will be a total loss. The Captain (Henry) and some 20 persons are saved. The *New Era* sailed from Bremerhaven on the 28th of September. The sea is high and every exertion is being made to save more of the passengers.[1]

During the time that she and Antupit were working on the book together, she was seeing Paul Desmond, the saxophonist for the Dave Brubeck Octet and later for Brubeck's Quartet, for which he wrote their hit "Take Five." Gloria and Paul lived in the same neighborhood and met at the corner deli. They enjoyed each other's sense of humor; however, the relationship did not last long. Desmond saw himself as merely the rebound relationship. Yet, as was the rule with her breakups, Gloria and Desmond remained friends until his premature death at age 52 in 1977.

By the time *The Beach Book* was published, Gloria was already in another relationship with Tom Guinzberg, the publisher of Viking Press. Guinzberg was well connected, eight years older than Gloria, and full of charm. Viking had published many famous authors, and Guinzberg was able to introduce her into intellectual as well as celebrity circles. He also lavished her with gifts such as expensive watches and trips to Paris.

Gloria's ability to move in any social circle has always been one of her potent qualities and she was well liked by many luminaries, including John Kenneth Galbraith, John Steinbeck, and Arthur Miller. She had an air of self-confidence that allowed her to mingle and take advantage of networking opportunities.

Networking is an important aspect of professional freelance writing, although nonwriters often forget that writing is a business like any other. Contacts help improve chances for contracts; however, writers are not handed work merely because they know someone. Once they are presented with an opportunity, they must present publishable work. Gloria thought of herself as a merely competent writer and once remarked, "I was good enough; I was publishable."[2] By 1963, she was writing regularly for *Glamour* magazine, as well as for *Esquire* and *Show*, and the contacts she made through Tom Guinzberg were invaluable.

A BUNNY'S TALE

This same year, during an editorial brainstorm meeting at *Show*, Gloria jokingly suggested that they hire someone to infiltrate the Playboy empire by posing as a Playboy Bunny for a while in order to report the pitfalls of the seemingly glamorous life. Her idea was flippant, directed toward *Show*'s publisher—Huntington Hartford, heir to the A&P Supermarkets fortune. He seemed to be in a type of competition with Hugh Hefner and *Playboy* magazine, and *Show*'s staff secretly scoffed at the rivalry. Gloria was not serious.

Her wry sense of humor had just opened the proverbial box of bad matter for herself, as the entire staff thought it was a great idea and that Gloria, tall and beautiful—perfect *Playboy* material—was the only writer at the magazine who might be able to complete the assignment. She read *Playboy*'s ad, telling her that if she was pretty, between ages 21 and 24, was able to be personable, and married or single, she could be a considered. Applicants needed no experience and if they fit the stated criteria, would probably qualify. Thinking that she was nearing 30, she hoped that *Playboy* would not accept her as a Bunny and reluctantly took the assignment.

Aside from her age, Gloria had another obstacle to overcome. To serve alcoholic beverages in New York, she would need identification. She did not want to use her real name; so, Gloria used her grandmother's name, Marie Catherine Ochs, because she still had a piece of identification bearing that name. Armed with her bogus name and wearing her most dramatic clothes, she went off to the Playboy Club for her interview.

After filling out her application and taking off her coat for a physical inspection, the matron in charge asked Gloria if she was really 24 years old. Gloria told the woman that she was, hoping to get in just under the wire. The woman looked her over and then said that she would make an appointment for her with the Bunny Mother for the following Wednesday evening.

She went back to the Bunnies' dressing room that Wednesday evening amidst a flurry of teased hair, net stockings, false eyelashes, and make-up, donning a half-clothed warren of young Bunnies preparing for their night's work. After an hour of waiting and watching the Bunnies' unusual procedures such as stuffing their costumes to make their bosoms appear larger, she was finally admitted to the Bunny Mother's office. When the woman saw Gloria, she asked her again if she was actually 24 years old. Gloria assured her that she was, and the woman said she looked much younger. Then, immediately, the Bunny Mother went into creating Gloria, the Playboy Bunny.

GLORIA'S TRANSFORMATION

Gloria was handed an old, royal blue satin costume rather like a one-piece bathing suit, with high French-cut legs and a strapless, plunging neckline, which was so tight that Gloria's skin caught when the woman pulled up the zipper. Gloria held her breath, and the second zip attempt was successful. To enhance her bosom, the Bunny Mother stuffed an entire cleaning bag (a thin plastic bag used to protect clothes after they have been dry-cleaned) into the top of Gloria's costume. Next, a blue band with the famous Bunny ears was placed on her head and a white cotton puff the size of a softball was attached to hooks at the bottom rear of the costume. A starched white collar with a clip-on bow tie, starched white cuffs with Playboy cuff links, and a pair of highheels would complete the outfit, though the cuffs and collar were withheld until she was officially accepted. The last touch would be her name tag set atop a round, ruffled trophy ribbon with streamers, which was pinned to the costume at the right hip, akin to the blue ribbon one might see at a county fair.

Once prepared, Gloria was escorted to her final interview. The woman looked at Gloria and asked if she wanted to be a Bunny, and Gloria told her that she did very much. That was it. She was hired without any background check or other interviews. She had passed the appearance test and was told to come back for a formal fitting for her own costume.

Gloria was permitted to keep the royal blue costume, and an orange costume was made specifically to fit her measurements. The costume's up-keep would cost her $2.50 per day. She also had to pay $5.00 a pair for thin, black tights and was given swatches of material from each costume and expected to have shoes dyed to match. The heels also had to be three inches high. All of the costume had to be in prime condition on any given night of the week, or the Bunnies suffered demerits, an accumulation of which could lead to employment termination.

BUNNY WAYS

After dressing, Gloria went to the Bunny Mother's office and received her Bunny bible and a four-page application. She made up most of the an-swers on the application and left the social security number blank. She was told to bring her card the following day and froze. The fictitious Marie Catherine Ochs had none. She simply told the woman that she would send home to Michigan for it and hoped it would take a while for them to discover that she was making everything up as she went along. However, in New York, she would not be allowed to serve alcoholic beverages or work late hours without identification to prove her age. She figured her tenure as a Bunny would be limited, but she filled out the usual tax infor-mation forms anyway, scheduled a complete physical with the Playboy physician, and signed up for rounds of training over the next few days. She would train on the floor within one week.

At her makeup lesson, she was fitted for a pair of fake eyelashes, which cost her $8.14 and were three-fourths of an inch long at their shortest point. While reading her Bunny bible, she learned that she would be ex-pected to make personal appearances but would not be paid for them. Bunnies were encouraged to sell drinks through pleasant interaction with the customers, who were mostly men, and a nightly prize was awarded to the Bunny who sold the most drinks. Yet, Bunnies were never to date club members and would be monitored by a detective agency to ensure that they did not. In fact, agency personnel were instructed to act as club key holders[3] and to proposition Bunnies by offering them as much as $200 to meet outside the club. Hugh Hefner was adamant about the Bunnies holding themselves and the club in high regard and forbade such behav-ior. Any Bunny who accepted such offers was summarily dismissed.

Gloria also learned about different Bunny types, including door Bun-nies, who greeted customers at the door; table Bunnies, who had to memorize a myriad of drinks; camera Bunnies, who took instant pictures of the guests with other Bunnies; cigarette Bunnies, who sold cigarettes and Playboy lighters; hatcheck Bunnies, who took care of members' coats; gift shop Bunnies, who sold Playboy merchandise from the gift store; and mobile gift shop Bunnies, who carried Playboy products from table to table.

Gloria was instructed on the finer points of the job at the lecture from the Bunny Mother. The girls received a $50 a week salary in accordance with New York minimum wage laws. The club took 50 percent of the first $30 in tips that customers charged to their accounts, 25 percent of tips up to $60, and 5 percent of amounts exceeding that limit. Bunnies were permitted to keep 100 percent of any cash tips paid to them, although they were forbidden to suggest to customers that tips be paid in cash. Boyfriends or husbands were not permitted to meet their Bunnies within two blocks of the club, as Playboy did not want customers to see Bunnies meeting other men.

Number One key holders, who were corporation presidents, celebrities, important members of the press, and other VIPs, were afforded very special treatment. Not only were these men pampered inside the club, but also Bunnies were permitted to give them their last names, to date them, and even to use the facilities of the club when in a Number One's company.

Bunnies were not permitted to bring men to any parties sponsored by Playboy. Management assured the women that dating and attending parties was not mandatory, but those who did not participate would surely be overlooked when better jobs were available.

WORKING THE FLOOR

Gloria's first job was as emergency hatcheck Bunny. Another Bunny had not shown up for work and a woman over 21 was needed to work the late hours. Gloria fit the bill and was told to tell the lobby director how much of her own money she had already stuffed into her suit, since hatcheck Bunnies were not allowed to retain tips. (Bunnies were not permitted to leave money in their lockers, either, so they carried cash in their costumes in a space between their breasts.) She was then thrust into a crowd of clamoring men who were waiting to hang up their coats. She was told she would be paid a flat $12 for eight hours work that evening. When Gloria suggested the wage would not equal the $300 a week that the ad for Bunnies offered, she was told that she would make up the difference when waiting tables, where keeping tips was allowed.

After five hours' work, Gloria's feet ached from her high heels, her fingers were sore from pushing pins through ID tags on coats, and she was frozen from the icy blasts coming through the front door each time it opened. She asked for a break and was given one-half hour to eat and no more. Every minute late would cost her one demerit. In the employee cafeteria, Gloria was permitted one free meal a day. She learned from other employees that beef stew was the menu every day, except on Fridays when they had fish. Most Bunnies snuck food for themselves from the members' buffet; however, if caught doing so, the penalty would be dismissal.

When she finally finished her night in the coat room, Gloria went to the dressing room to change her costume. Welts from the costume's zipper appeared on her spine and indentations showed from the stays underneath her bosom. Her feet ached horribly and she offhandedly mentioned the tightness of the costume to another Bunny in the dressing room with her. The woman told her she was lucky, as some women's costumes caused their thighs to go numb. On her way out the employee entrance, to top off the evening, Gloria was propositioned by a cab driver who saw her leave the club. Some men took it for granted that if a girl was a Playboy Bunny, she might be a prostitute as well. Gloria declined the ride and walked back to her apartment.

Training for table Bunny was early the next afternoon, and due to a shortage that night, Gloria found herself actually waiting tables. Her first customer handed her his key, which avowed his membership, and along with it a key to his hotel. Performing the famous Bunny Dip, whereby the woman bends her knees slightly, points her right hip to the table, and leans slightly backward, Gloria gave both keys back to the gentleman politely.

The following day she set out early so she could casually interview a few of the Bunnies for her article. She was interested in seeing how many of them were college students. She offhandedly asked what they had wanted to do before becoming Bunnies and what they would do afterward. Most wanted to be models, mainly advertising models (as opposed to runway models), and saw Bunnying as a road to that end. Others wanted to meet nice members and get married. She was told there were some college girls, but they only worked weekends. Another Bunny had been a secretary and opted to try Bunnying for an increase in earnings. Gloria was able to share dancing experience with another girl, and another was a mother with a baby just trying to earn extra money for the family.

That night, with borrowed shoes three sizes too big to accommodate her swollen feet from the night before and her ribs wrapped in gauze to ease the pain of the costume, Gloria hit the floor, once again. She was assigned to the Living Room, as she had been the night before, in the Cartoon Corner, where Playboy cartoons adorned the walls—a very difficult station due to its distance from the bar and set of steps she would have to go up and down all evening.

After she had worked the entire weekend, she had to return to the club for publicity photos on Sunday. No one had asked about her identification, and it seemed as though she could work as long as she liked, regardless of the situation. She decided to stay until the following Friday. That night, she told the Bunny Mother that she had to quit to take care of her ailing mother.

One day shy of three weeks as a Bunny, Gloria worried that her arches might be falling and in her article, "I Was a Playboy Bunny," she wrote in diary form that her feet ached like rotten teeth and were swollen so much that she could not get her shoes on. Each night that she had served her own station, she traveled between tables and bar 16 times an hour on average, and on the first night alone had had three drinks spilled down her back. She had lost 10 pounds and was paid for the nights she had waited a station, but not for her work in the checkroom, as the club considered that part of her unpaid training. Her first week's wages amounted to $35.90 after taxes.

FINDING FAME

Gloria's article "I Was a Playboy Bunny" propelled her to instant fame. However, in her eyes not all of the publicity was positive. She was suddenly thrust into the role of the attractive woman who wrote the article rather than the role of the writer who happened to be an attractive woman. She received letters from women asking for advice on how to become Playboy Bunnies and was often introduced as an ex-Bunny. This impression of her as a femme fatal rather than journalist, caused her to return money advanced to a paperback book publisher, who wanted her to write a book about the experience. The whole thing had gone in a direction Gloria had never intended to take.

She was also sued by Playboy for $1 million because a small New York newspaper had printed a report on the article and had alleged that the New York Playboy Club manager had mafia connections. Although Gloria had never published that information or even reported it, she was dragged into the suit as well. She had many unpleasant deposition sessions through which she was cleared of any wrongdoing. The newspaper settled out of court.

Yet, the publicity surrounding the article and litigation paid off in other ways. By the end of 1963, she had done several major magazine interviews and became a celebrity. She was well ensconced in the New York writing scene and able to secure writing assignments on a regular basis. Although the projects were not as meaty as she had hoped they would be, at least she was writing and becoming known. Also that year, *The Beach Book* was mentioned favorably as an entertaining read in *Vogue's* "People Are Talking" column.

Aside from Tom Guinzberg, who Gloria was still seeing, other friends helped her meet influential people and make invaluable contacts as well. Earlier in 1963, she had met Ted Sorensen, aide to President John F. Kennedy and the man who penned the famous, "And so, my fellow Americans: ask not what your country can do for you—ask what you can do for your country," for Kennedy's inaugural speech and also ghost wrote Kennedy's *Profiles in Courage*. Author James C. Humes described him thusly: "Although Sorensen was a lawyer by profession, he had a poet's love for and fascination with words and their sounds. At parties the introverted, bespectacled legislative aide would amuse guests with rhyming ditties."[4] Not only did the couple have writing in common, but they also felt an instant bond as products of unusual childhoods. Gloria wrote of their relationship: "I once fell in love with a man only because we both belonged to that large and secret club of children who had 'crazy mothers.'"[5]

Nearing the end of 1963 and during their relationship, major societal changes were imminent, and at the forefront was Betty Friedan and *The Feminine Mystique*, which was published that January. Her opus on the oppression felt by everyday suburban wives and mothers rocked the world and would one day, in turn, rock Gloria's.

HOUSEWIVES DISCOVER THEIR DISCONTENT

Marrying a doctor was quite the achievement for women in 1963 and considered by many to be a pinnacle of success. Doctors' wives, lawyers' wives, and other suburban housewives had it all—beautiful houses, beautiful children, beautiful clothes, and beautiful cars. They cooked lovely meals for their families, kept lovely homes, and joined the lovely PTA. Life was wonderful for the 93 percent of all American women in their 30s who were married with families. Or was it?

Some women realized that they were living only to serve others. Of course, serving others is a worthy pursuit, and some women were pleasantly pleased with their station in life; yet, others had epiphanies—they wanted more and were unhappy with the status quo. Many of them sought solace in tranquilizers, prescribed by their family physician, or in alcohol. And while they suffered, others wondered how they could be so unhappy, considering all they had.

Betty Friedan was the first woman to write about these feelings of this era in *The Feminine Mystique*:

> The problem lay buried, unspoken, for many years in the minds of American women. It was a strange stirring, a sense of dissatisfaction, a yearning that women suffered in the middle of the twentieth century in the United States. Each suburban wife struggled with it alone. As she made the beds, shopped for groceries, matched slipcover material, ate peanut butter sandwiches with her children, chauffeured Cub Scouts and Brownies, lay beside her husband at night—she was afraid to ask even of herself the silent question—Is this all?[6]

Was it all, indeed? Women read Friedan's book and it started a revolution. Women realized for the first time that they were not the only unhappy, perfect wife and mother, but many other women in their places had the same feelings. The realization that each person gets only one life, and that in that life, it is only fair that a person has something of his or her own—something to be proud of or to have accomplished—became clear. Many college educated women were in this group and their feelings of being held back by a male dominated society were poised to explode.

A series of life altering changes for our nation continued, on November 22, 1963, when President Kennedy was assassinated in Dallas, Texas. Grief not only overwhelmed his advisor, Ted Sorensen, but also Gloria and the entire nation. The Kennedys represented a time of strength and hope in America, and the Camelot of King Arthur was often used as a metaphor for Kennedy's administration. When the President was shot, the dream ended and the entire nation sensed it.

MOVING ON AGAIN

As Ted Sorensen was quite close to Jack Kennedy, he was hard hit by the assassination. Gloria, who was working in New York City, was not able to type Sorensen an E-mail or call him on a cell phone, and state-to-state long distance calls were still quite expensive. So, Gloria consoled him through letters and offered support in any way she could from afar, but she already knew that nothing would keep them together, and soon after, the relationship ended due to Sorensen's traditional values. Of that conflict, she wrote, "I fell out of love when he confessed that he wished I wouldn't smoke or swear, and he hoped I wouldn't go on working."[7] Apparently still needing support, Sorensen married another woman shortly afterward, but the union did not last.

Gloria was rarely, if ever, alone; so no breakup was devastating to her. She had a series of easy letdowns and usually remained lifelong friends with the men she had dated. But most men she met loved her for her charm, intelligence, wit, and dancer's grace. They also loved her look, which was lean and sexy but with a touch of class. And she was not threatening. She was always centered, regardless of what life threw at her, partly an inheritance from her father and partly because she had taken the adult role at 11 years old. Although Gloria was assertive in her goals, she was not aggressive, and men found these qualities enthralling.

Gloria was still writing and soon found a new relationship. Also through Tom Guinzberg, Gloria had met director Mike Nichols, who was an instant success on Broadway through the play *Barefoot in the Park*, which he had directed in 1963. As they dated, she met many celebrities such as Mike's former comedy team partner Elaine May and a young Julie Andrews, who was just starting her career. Gloria and Mike attended President Lyndon B. Johnson's inauguration together. At the same time as she was seeing Nichols, knowing that she never intended to marry, Gloria also saw other men as a potential doorway out of her current relationship. With a man as high profile as Nichols, she felt she would be living his life rather than her own, and the relationship did not last.

At the same time, Gloria's own spotlight was waxing. In February, *Glamour* published a long piece, emphasizing her looks—her clothes and makeup. Yet, Gloria wanted to be known for her mind and her ability to write seriously; she wanted to be recognized and validated. Still, the media continued to concentrate on her appearance and her article about Playboy Bunnies. Yet, as in the old adage, any publicity is good PR. Gloria was earning name and face recognition that would benefit her in a cause she had not yet discovered.

NOTES

1. Steinem, *The Beach Book*, pp. 266–67.
2. Quoted in Heilbrun, *Education of a Woman*, p. 104.

3. Membership in the Playboy Club was identified by the rabbit-headed, metal Playboy Key, which was switched to a plastic key card in 1966.

4. Humes, *My Fellow Americans*, p. 218.

5. Steinem, *Outrageous Acts*, p. 162.

6. Betty Friedan, *The Feminine Mystique* (New York: W. W. Norton & Co., 1963; reprint, 1983), p. 15 (page citation is to the reprint edition).

7. Steinem, *Outrageous Acts*, p. 162.

Chapter 8

PUSHING THE POLITICAL

As Sorensen and Guinzberg faded from Gloria's life, Herb Sargent, whom she had met on double dates with Guinzberg, faded in. He had by this time won an Emmy for Outstanding Writing Achievement in Comedy, Variety, or Music for *Annie, The Women in the Life of a Man* and was the head writer for *That Was the Week That Was*, lovingly known as *TW3*, the American version of a program begun in the United Kingdom in 1962, which was hosted by British TV personality, producer and writer David Frost.

The American version of *TW3*, which aired on NBC, poked fun at current events through skits, songs, and one-liners and included performances by actors Alan Alda, Henry Morgan, Buck Henry, Phyllis Newman, as well as special correspondent David Frost from the UK. The show had been picked up as a midseason replacement for the 1963–64 term, and Sargent asked Gloria to write for a department of the show entitled "Surrealism in Everyday Life," in which she would satirize odd statistics. Her first Surrealism Awards appeared on the January 19, 1965 show, and the last would appear in April of that year when the show was cancelled.

But important events had occurred that were shaping a new world by 1964, events that would have heavy bearing on Gloria's life. In December 1961, President Kennedy had established the President's Commission on the Status of Women in response to a proposal by Esther Peterson, director of the Women's Bureau and later Assistant Secretary of Labor. He instructed the committee to study federal employment and wage policies and practices, federal and state labor laws, and the civil rights of women, among other issues, and to report back to him by October 1963. Former First Lady Eleanor Roosevelt was to chair the 25-member commission, 14 of whom were women. Acknowledging the goals of the commission, all government department heads were to review policies concerning the hiring of women.

Because of this study, three actions were taken. In April 1962, in all civil service promotions, women were to be considered equally with men. In July, all executive department heads received a memo from the president, insisting that all promotions were to be made based on individual merit, without regard to sex, color, or religion. Also important to furthering the rights of women, the president signed into law the Equal Pay Act, guaranteeing equal pay to women working for any company subject to the Fair Labor Standards Act.

Although this was a solid beginning, the Commission found that women were discriminated against in virtually every facet of life and produced their report *American Women*.[1] However, the Commission fell short of endorsing the Equal Rights Amendment (ERA), which was introduced in Congress in 1923 as the Lucretia Mott Amendment, and read: "Men and women shall have equal rights throughout the United States and every place subject to its jurisdiction." The amendment, although introduced in every session of Congress up to that point, had failed to pass, and the Commission was not eager to undermine their findings by including the issue.

Continuing the work begun by the Kennedy administration, Congress passed the Civil Rights Act in July 1964, which included a provision to prevent discrimination in the workplace. Section 703 (a) read, in part:

> (a) It shall be an unlawful employment practice for an employer—
> (1) to fail or refuse to hire or to discharge any individual, or otherwise to discriminate against any individual with respect to his compensation, terms, conditions, or privileges of employment, because of such individual's race, color, religion, sex, or national origin; or
> (2) to limit, segregate, or classify his employees in any way which would deprive or tend to deprive any individual of employment opportunities or otherwise adversely affect his status as an employee, because of such individual's race, color, religion, sex, or national origin.[2]

Not only did the new legislation open closed doors for people of color, but for women, who theretofore had not been treated fairly in the workplace, and the Equal Employment Opportunity Commission (EEOC) was established to enforce the law. With a level playing field, women's roles were poised to change. History professor Mary Frances Berry wrote, "When the Civil Rights Act of 1964, Title VII, to end race discrimination in employment came before the Congress, the results gave impetus to the developing women's rights movement. Women reformers played key roles in amending the legislation to cover sex discrimination."[3] However, changes in perception take a great deal of time to change, and the efficacy of the law would not be felt for several more years.

STRIVING FOR THE PLUM ASSIGNMENT

Writing continued to be the biggest part of Gloria's independent life throughout 1965. For *Glamour*, she wrote "A Day in Chicago with Saul Bellow," and she did another profile of author James Baldwin for *Vogue*, among several other profiles of renowned talent. She saw herself as particularly suited to the occupation and wrote, "For me, writing is the only thing that passes the three tests of métier: first, when I'm doing it, I don't feel that I should be doing something else; second, it produces a sense of accomplishment and, once in a while, pride; and third, it's frightening."[4]

Gloria continued to shine in the spotlight, and in 1965, other publications continued their exploration of her. *Newsday* did an article about her entitled "The World's Most Beautiful Byline," and *Newsweek* titled their piece "News Girl." The Bunny article had propelled her into celebrity and her looks managed to keep her there. People, especially women, were intrigued by her attractiveness and impressed by her talent. Gloria became an early role model for women, as she worked in a man's world and was succeeding.

She was still not part of the women's movement, however interested she may have been. In June, the Third National Conference on Commissions on the Status of Women was held in Washington, D.C., and among its participants was Betty Friedan. On June 30, furious over the EEOC's failure to enforce Title VII of the Civil Rights Act, Friedan invited some women from the conference to her hotel room to discuss other options aside from passing a resolution recommending this enforcement. Freidan wrote, "Most didn't think women needed a movement like the blacks, but everyone was mad at the sabotage of Title VII."[5]

The only solution seemed to be the formation of a new organization, which would be dedicated to the attainment of full equality for women. Friedan christened it the National Organization for Women (NOW) and the group drafted this statement of purpose: "To take action to bring women into full participation in the mainstream of American society now, assuming all the privileges and responsibilities thereof in fully equal partnership with men."[6] With a startup budget of $140, NOW was born, and in October, the group held its first organizational meeting at the John Phillips Sousa Community Room of the Washington Post Building, in order to form its hierarchy and philosophy, with more than 300 men and women attending. During the meeting, Friedan was elected president and Kathryn Clarenbach was elected first board chairperson, and NOW's first task forces were established in the realms of family life, education, employment, media, religion, women in poverty, and women's legal and political rights.

Gloria did not consider herself to be part of the NOW society. Of course, she understood and sympathized with the fight, but was a woman in control of her own life, not controlled by any man. She felt she could offer the organization little and vice versa.

As her career continued its upward climb, in 1966, Gloria had her first encounters with the film industry. Robbie Wald, the son of movie producer Jerry Wald, hired Gloria to write a modern version of a property titled *High Heels*, a story surrounding a dance hall girl. Gloria changed the lead character's status to that of a dancer in a topless bar, changed the title to *Cally*, and spent endless hours interviewing topless dancers all over the city of Los Angeles. Wald wanted to produce the project himself, but as he was an unproven manager, the deal collapsed.

RUBBING ELBOWS WITH THE RICH AND FAMOUS WHILE ROME SMOLDERS

Resuming her print writing career, Gloria would interview author Truman Capote for *Glamour* that year and was subsequently invited to his famous Black and White Ball scheduled for November 28 at the Plaza Hotel. In the wake of Capote's very successful book about the murder of a Kansas family, *In Cold Blood*, the party was ostensibly thrown for Kathryn Graham, publisher of the *Washington Post*. The gala was touted by some as the Party of the Decade. Capote had spent a whole summer planning it and insisted upon the guests wearing black and white dress with an exotic mask. Only the cream of society was invited, and the guest list included author Norman Mailer; Lee Radziwill, the sister of Jacqueline Kennedy Onassis; historian Arthur Schlesinger, Jr.; political analyst William F. Buckley, Jr.; and actors Tallulah Bankhead, Candice Bergen, Mia Farrow, and her then husband, singer Frank Sinatra. Everyone reported having a wonderful time, and Norman Mailer remembered calling political advisor

McGeorge Bundy out to fight over the Vietnam War. Still, everyone talked about the party for years, and the event was even included in the December 26, 1999, New York Times article "10 Parties That Shook the Century," in which Penelope Green wrote, "It was...probably the purest example of what can be called the [producer-director] Irwin Allen-Towering Inferno theory of party-giving: cram as many bold-face names into as large a space as will hold them."[7] Once again, Gloria was interjected into a sea of famous faces, and her own had become one of them.

Yet, in the background, a black cloud was forming. *Ramparts* magazine, which began as a monthly magazine for progressive Catholics covering church and secular affairs, had been transformed under the auspices of Warren Hinckle, who became its editor in 1967. Suddenly, *Ramparts* was about politics and social issues, affecting not only Catholics but all Americans. Ramparts soon broke one scoop after another.

In an early incendiary piece, *Ramparts* uncovered facts that proved the National Student Association (NSA), which had become the largest student association in the country, had been funded by the CIA since 1952, and a fury over this information began. Political analyst and writer Max Holland wrote:

> A rash of stories quickly followed as elite news outlets raced to outdo the upstart *Ramparts* by exposing a variety of covert CIA subsidies to private organizations in the United States and abroad. The agency seemed to have its tentacles inside every sector of American society: student and teacher groups, labor unions, foundations, legal and business organizations, even universities. The disclosures lent substance to the criticism that the CIA was nothing less than an invisible government.[8]

This disclosure was part of the progressive unrest in the American population. The Vietnam War had claimed nearly 20,000 American lives in its first 10 years, and as the first war to be televised, images of the carnage in Southeast Asia were channeled to the American public on a daily basis. Blood and death being pumped into their living rooms alarmed the American people as never before. Americans began to question the validity of the war in Vietnam and teach-ins, which educated college students about the war, had raised not only their consciousness, but also their outrage. In April of 1967 huge demonstrations against the war and racial discrimination gathered thousands of protesters in Washington, D.C., and New York City, where they listened to speakers such as Martin Luther King, Jr. and Dr. Benjamin Spock.

GROWING NATIONAL UNREST

Gloria demonstrated against the war with the Women's Strike for Peace coalition, where she met Bella Abzug, an attorney who championed and practiced in civil rights and labor law, and who for the first time, was a woman with whom Gloria would come to have a close and lasting relationship. Yet, she was not pleased with the outcome of the demonstration and wrote, "I got discouraged after a Washington trip with Women Strike for Peace because they somehow ended up speaking only to more or less friends (Robert Kennedy, Jacob Javits) about the uselessness of the war, and booing *them*."[9]

Aside from the war, 1967 was a time of free expression, drugs, free love, and hippies. LSD and the smell of marijuana burning could be found on campuses all around the United States. Be-ins, where masses of young people frolicked, ingested drugs in mass quantities, and listened to the Jefferson Airplane band and the Ike and Tina Turner Revue, took place at the Polo Grounds in Golden Gate Park, San Francisco, in January and in June at the Monterey Pop Festival with musicians such as Janis Joplin and the Grateful Dead performing. That season was dubbed the Summer of Love, but the whole thrust of the message was change—material and massive changes to break completely away from the norm. The times were encapsulated in Dr. Timothy Leary's coined phrase, "Turn on, tune in, and drop out."[10] Unhappy with the status quo, the elders of the Boomer generation, largely comprised of people born between 1946 and 1964, had decided that the country needed reshaping.

African Americans were also eager to change the status quo, after years of oppression that began with slavery. Racial tensions were high in 1967 and in July, Cleveland, Newark, and Detroit exploded in rioting. Carol Schmidt, a white reporter for the *Michigan Chronicle*, an African American weekly in Detroit between 1965 and 1968, remembered those times and wrote:

> The kitchen window of my apartment overlooked Tenth Precinct, where the first rioters were taken, and I had to show ID to get into my apartment since I could have shot into the station from my window. A tank, yes, a tank, was in my parking lot. Storefronts a few hundred feet from me were on fire, and the smoke throughout the city choked us all. People were looting all over the city, including friends I would have never dreamed would jump at the opportunity to get back at the store owners who they felt had exploited them for years. Stores,

which identified themselves as black-owned, were not hit except where the fires spread uncontrollably.

I drove into downtown each day and was shot at along the way, through the smoke and crazy National Guard troops who were far more terrifying than the rioters who were my neighbors. At night, I slept on a mattress pulled into the bathroom, which had at least two walls all around and therefore felt more safe from the erratic shots that went on all night. I wrote several articles for the *National Catholic Reporter* about the riots during the same time, typing while sitting on the toilet, hoping the sound of the typewriter would not be mistaken for gunfire.[11]

These situations undoubtedly got Gloria's attention, as she was bent on writing about politics. She was already leaning toward this type of writing in a new venture with an old friend—Clay Felker. There had always been a power struggle at *Esquire* between Felker, who wanted the magazine to reflect service journalism to give readers useful information, and Harold Hayes, who leaned toward idea-driven journalism, where stories are often tailored to prove a writer's preexisting thesis. Felker saw service journalism as the way of the future.

Felker left *Esquire* in 1962, and knowing he needed a job, Gloria persuaded Tom Guinzberg to hire Felker as a consultant for Viking Press, which in turn lead to consulting for the Sunday edition of the *Herald Tribune*. Felker would launch a new magazine for the Sunday edition of the paper entitled *New York*. Among those who wrote for the supplement were such writing luminaries as Jimmy Breslin, Liz Smith, Walt Kelly, and Peter Maas. Felker also included Gloria in the new venture.

Felker and Gloria never had a romantic relationship. He prized her—not for her good looks, although he undoubtedly was charmed by her. He loved her intellect and talent. She was a smart woman, and they were colleagues, writers with intensity, verve, and élan.

CREATING HER NICHE

By 1966, Gloria was helping Felker to find outside financing to turn *New York* into a stand-alone publication, and she remembers many luncheons with the purpose of fund-raising. In return for her help, Felker saw to it that Gloria was paid stock in the magazine for the work she had done. And with the funding in hand, they set out to establish a working environment and a staff, which continued throughout 1967. By the end of that year, she was also writing a regular column—"The City Politic"—and she was finally a serious journalist writing her passions for politics.

Gloria was beginning her political writing career at a volatile time. By 1967, the Vietnam War was in full swing and demonstrations were breaking out all over the country. A New Left had formed aside a New Right. Both movements, seated in the youth sector, challenged the status of the old guard liberals and stressed grass roots politics. Yet, the two factions were antagonistic toward each other. As author Jonathan Martin Kolkey described the animosity: "The New Left condemned the New Rightists as bluenoses, prudes, religious fanatics, trigger-happy militarists, racists, and anti-Semites. In the eyes of the New Left, the New Right represented an American Fascist Movement. Conversely, the New Right denounced the New Leftists as sexual deviates, drug addicts, atheists, effeminate cowards, and race mongrelizers. From the outset, the New Right viewed the New Left as Communist-inspired, -financed, and -directed."[12] Loosely allied with the New Left were the antiwar movement people and the Black Panthers, militants striving for racial equality. The whole mélange was roiling, threatening to erupt.

Gloria was doing her part to protest through the Writers and Editors War Tax Protest of 1968. Begun by Gerald Walker of *New York Times Magazine*, it entailed withholding tax payment to protest the 10 percent war surtax imposed by the federal government in that year; 528 editors and writers participated, one of whom was Gloria Steinem. Although most daily papers refused to carry an ad for the protest, *Ramparts*, the *New York Post*, and the *New York Review of Books* agreed. Some writers and editors had determined that 23 percent of their income had been designated for the war in Vietnam and vowed to withhold an even larger amount.

April 1968 also saw Gloria's first political article in the first stand-alone issue of *New York*, and her interest in politics and her work meshed for the first time. Yet, almost immediately after the premiere issue of *New York* hit the stands, civil rights leader Dr. Martin Luther King, Jr. was assassinated by a sniper on April 4 in Memphis, Tennessee. He had traveled to Memphis to lend support to striking sanitation workers, a majority of whom were black, and hoped to help the city avoid another violent confrontation. Fighting had already broken out between strikers, supporters, and police. But King had begun to lose supporters for his nonviolent movement and had come under attack by not only the white conservatives, but by black power advocates and even moderates, unhappy with his antiwar philosophy. On the night of his speech, he had already received 50 death threats.

According to authors Maurice Isserman and Michael Kazin, "News of the murder, committed by an escaped white convict named James Earl Ray, convinced thousands of black people that the present was damnable enough. They poured into the streets of over 120 cities to express grief and rage in a spasm of collective violence."[13] San Francisco's Haight-Ashbury district and Washington, D.C., saw some of the worst looting and violence in American history. And in New York, Gloria was sent to cover the melee for *New York* magazine. For several days, Gloria and Lloyd Weaver, a young black writer, followed Mayor John Lindsay around the city as he went from New York community to community, showing black people he cared. Because of his compassion, New York stayed relatively calm.

Along with the fabric of American society, the political scene was set to change again. Earlier that year, on March 31, due to the misery from Vietnam and American unrest, Lyndon Johnson had decided not to seek nomination in the 1968 presidential election. He had nearly been beaten in the New Hampshire primary by presidential candidate Eugene Mc-Carthy on March 12, and Robert Kennedy had announced his candidacy four days later. Johnson knew it would be a tough fight, and Vietnam had become the bane of his term in office. Casualties mounted, and so did the number of troops "in country." Protests were cropping up throughout the Western world and often ended in violence and sometimes death. At the end of April, students and antiwar supporters occupied five buildings on the Columbia University campus, and the action ended with police storming the buildings to forcibly remove the protesters at the administration's request.

MARCHING FOR MIGRANTS

Also taking action around this time was Cesar Chavez, a man from El Paso, Texas, who could no longer stand to see the conditions that migrant farm workers were subjected to in the United States. Mexican immigrants, desperate to stay in America, were willing to drive hundreds of miles, from farm to farm, and put up with almost anything to make a living. Author Stephen S. Sosnick, Professor of Agricultural Economics at the University of California, Davis, reported, "The investigations and hearings [in California] established a number of points: field workers seldom had access to latrines or hand washing facilities, often drank water from a shared vessel, and occasionally lacked potable water to drink."[14]

In 1962, Chavez began traveling from camp to camp, asking workers to join a union. Dolores Huerta joined Chavez in this drive, and after six months, the National Farm Workers Association (NFWA), which later became the United Farm Workers Union (UFW), was founded with 300 members. At their first meeting in Fresno, California, La Causa (the cause) was born.

Gloria lent her support to La Causa, also in April 1968, after a telephone conversation with Marion Moses, who worked closely with Chavez. She had been successful in attaining interviews with *Time* and *Life* magazines, but had made little progress in fund raising. When Moses explained why she was calling, Gloria told her, "Of course, I'd like to help."[15] Her media contacts and ideas on raising money for La Causa were invaluable to the movement and she offered Moses a place to stay. Since union organizers were living on $5 a week, Moses was grateful for and accepted the offer.

When Cesar Chavez came to New York to make his appearances on television and in interviews, Gloria met him for the first time and afterward, helped plan a benefit at Carnegie Hall, along with Dolores Huerta. Even after the union people left New York and went back to California, Gloria continued to work for the cause.

PRELUDE TO THE 1968 DEMOCRATIC NATIONAL CONVENTION

Gloria had also begun to write about national electoral politics. Four candidates would run in the 1968 Democratic primary races—George McGovern, whom Gloria had met in 1965; Senator Eugene McCarthy, for whom she had written some campaign literature; Hubert Humphrey, the incumbent vice president; and Senator Robert Kennedy, to whom Gloria planned to switch her alliance. Yet, after winning the California primary on June 5, Kennedy was assassinated by a Jordanian militant, apparently angered by Kennedy's pro-Israel stance.

McCarthy won Gloria's allegiance after the assassination, and in order to do a cover story of him for *New York*, she traveled with his campaign for a few days and came away feeling less supportive. McCarthy's intellectualism and cold demeanor put her off and he seemed abysmally dull. Her story "Trying to Love Eugene" for *New York* was less than positive. Soon after, she took up the banner for George McGovern, who she once declared was the "real Eugene McCarthy."[16] However, McGovern had not yet declared his candidacy, but after persuasion from supporters, and as a replacement for Senator Kennedy, McGovern threw his hat into the ring on August 10. To help his campaign, Gloria wrote pamphlets and raised money. She also did a great deal of talking, helping people to see why McGovern would be the best choice, and arranged luncheons with editors at the *New York Times* and *Time* magazine. She even dressed him in clothes befitting a presidential candidate. McGovern admitted, "She sharpened me up."[17]

The best thing about Gloria for the candidate was that she was a great fund-raiser. When she offered to help with his campaign, McGovern chided, "Come with a bunch of money."[18] So, Gloria showed up with a check for $10,000, which she had obtained from a private individual.

To further her assistance, Gloria also attended the Democratic National Convention (DNC) in August as part of the McGovern party and later wrote about the scenes of violence that occurred there. On January 31, 1968, the Vietnamese New Year's Day, the North Vietnamese Army had launched a major offensive in South Vietnam, and it took weeks before United States and South Vietnamese soldiers were able to retake their positions, including the former imperial capital, Hue, and even the American embassy in Saigon. Up until this point, American officials had claimed that the war had already been won. Images flashing across the television sets in American homes showed that the war was not only still raging, but that troops had come dangerously close to being overrun.

U.S. SENTIMENT TURNS SOUR

In *The Tet Offensive*, editors Marc Jason Gilbert and William Head remarked, "The Tet Offensive caused one of the deepest and most lasting of the many rents that the Vietnam or Second Indochina War made in the fabric of American life: hence the reputation of that campaign as the Vietnam War's Vietnam. Americans have since come to regard it either as defining the moment when the United States seized defeat out of the jaws of victory, or as the wake-up call that finally alerted America to the unwinnable nature of the Vietnam conflict."[19]

Yet even before the Tet Offensive began, members of the Youth International Party (Yippies) Abbie Hoffman and Jerry Rubin had begun to plan demonstrations for the Democratic National Convention eight months hence in Chicago. In March, they came up with a name for their activities—The Festival of Life—and later that month David Dellinger, Rennie Davis, and Tom Hayden joined Hoffman and Rubin in planning the demonstrations. For the first time, Mobilization to End the War (MOBE), the Students for a Democratic Society (SDS—a radical antiwar, antigovernment group), and the Yippies banded together toward a common goal. Soon permits to demonstrate were submitted to the Chicago Parks Department and all were denied, except one allowing them to rally in Grant Park, just east of the Chicago Loop; however, officials declined to allow demonstrators to sleep in the parks overnight, and ultimately, an 11 P.M. curfew was installed.

On April 11, Congress was busy approving the Anti-Riot Act of 1968, to outlaw rioting in the streets because of the growing number of antiwar demonstrations, and making it a crime to cross state lines with the intention of starting a riot. Life as Americans knew it had ceased to exist. People from all lifestyles questioned the war in Vietnam, and the conflict between those opposed and loyalists had torn the country apart.

On August 23, the feathers finally hit the fan when organizers marched to the Conrad Hilton hotel in Chicago, the site of the DNC. Throughout convention week, arrests and violence broke out in various parts of the city, the worst occurring in Old Town and Lincoln Park. Yet, the television cameras, positioned near the Conrad Hilton, filmed police macing and clubbing demonstrators and bystanders when Deputy Police Superintendent James Rochford, at the behest of Mayor Richard Daley, ordered the police to clear the streets. Inside the International Amphitheater, Senator Abraham Ribicoff of Connecticut nominated George McGovern, while denouncing the "Gestapo tactics on the streets of Chicago."[20]

Although Gloria worked almost constantly, she saw the violence through the window of cramped hotel rooms, doubling for campaign headquarters. She also experienced the violence first hand when she was shoved aside and her glasses were broken as she handed out McGovern pamphlets on the convention floor. Yet, Gloria's selfless efforts were for naught, as incumbent Vice President Hubert H. Humphrey was chosen as the Democratic presidential candidate.

Continuing her political activism, in December of 1968, Gloria participated in a panel discussion, which included Jean Faust, the national legislative chairperson for NOW. Gloria brought up the idea that women were expected only to write about female issues, involving motherhood, children, makeup, and fashion, and Faust was so impressed that she asked Gloria to join in the feminist fight with NOW. Gloria refused, saying that although she sympathized with feminist ideals, she considered herself a humanist. Although Faust expected Gloria to reconsider at some point, no one was more surprised than Gloria when that moment arrived.

NOTES

1. Margaret Mead and Frances Balgley Kaplan, eds., *American Women: The Report of the President's Commission on the Status of Women and Other Publications of the Commission* (New York: Scribner's, 1965).

2. *Civil Rights Act of 1964*, Public Law 88–352, 88th Cong., 2nd sess. (2 July 1964).

3. Berry, *Why ERA Failed*, p. 61.

4. Steinem, *Outrageous Acts*, p. 14.

5. Friedan, *The Feminine Mystique*, p. 384 (reprint ed.).

6. "NOW's Past," *The National Organization of Women*, http://nownyc.org/past.htm.

7. Penelope Green, "10 Parties That Shook the Century," *New York Times*, 26 December 1999, sec. 9, p. 1.

8. Max Holland, "Was Jim Garrison Duped by the KGB?" *New Orleans*, February 2002, pp. 38–45.

9. Quoted in Heilbrun, *Education of a Woman*, pp. 130–31.

10. Ian Shoales, "Timothy Leary's Dead—Really, Three Decades Later, Moody Blues Vindicated," *Salon*, 31 May 1996, http://www.salon.com/weekly/leary960531.html.

11. Carol Schmidt, interview with author, 20 February 2003.

12. Kolkey, *The New Right*, p. 235.

13. Isserman and Kazin, *America Divided*, p. 227.

14. Sosnick, *Hired Hands*, p. 248.

15. Quoted in Heilbrun, *Education of a Woman*, p. 168.

16. Ibid., p. 163.

17. Ibid., p. 164.

18. Ibid., p. 164.

19. Gilbert and Head, *The Tet Offensive*, p. 1.

20. Dean Blobaum, "Chicago '68: A Chronology," *Chicago '68*, http://www.geocities.com/Athens/Delphi/1553/c68chron.html.

Chapter 9

EMERGING AS A FEMINIST

By 1969, a second wave of the Women's Movement had ignited a passion for feminine equality in cities all over the country. In addition to New York coalitions, groups sprang up in Chicago, Boston, Seattle, San Francisco, Pittsburgh, and Washington, D.C., between 1967 and 1969. Betty Friedan's NOW represented the moderate group, while radical groups were splintering away from New York Radical Women, who advocated growth through the proliferation of "leaderless/structureless groups of no more than 15"[1] members. As one historian wrote, "New groups proliferated when existing ones split over ideological or political matters or when they grew too large to sustain a participatory structure. The growth was called development by fission, a metaphor that conveyed the energy of a movement intent on changing both consciousness and society."[2]

Demonstrations had begun in 1968 when radicals marched at the Miss America pageant in Atlantic City. Around 200 women attended, carrying placards, singing, and throwing stereotypically feminine dishcloths, girdles, and bras into the fire—ergo, the term bra burners, which is often deprecatingly substituted for the term feminist.

The following year, the Plaza Hotel in Manhattan was the target of feminist attention and NOW planned a demonstration for February 12, 1969. Gloria had experienced discrimination there herself, and Jean Faust asked her to join, not knowing the embarrassment Gloria had suffered as a result of Plaza policies. Gloria had waited for an interview subject in the Plaza's lobby, but was told she would have to leave the premises, as unescorted women were not allowed, and was ushered out the door. She wrote, "I was humiliated: Did I look like a prostitute?"[3] She also missed her interview, since the actor she was to meet looked for her, did not see her, and called her editor to complain that Gloria never arrived.

Still, Gloria had no intention of joining the protest and begged off politely. She had no interest in alliance with the group and saw *The Feminine Mystique* geared toward mostly white, middle-class women living in the suburbs. Though she helped other women whenever she could, especially in business, she had no interest in protesting for the right to luncheon in the Oak Room of the Plaza without a man. She felt that mainstream society viewed these women in a negative light, as frivolous middle-class white women with nothing better to do. Even then, she realized that the first feminists of the second wave—as opposed to the first wave feminists, who fought for women's suffrage—were breaking barriers for working-class women on factory assembly lines; and she feared that storming the Oak Room, a highly expensive eatery, would only misrepresent the image of the women's movement more than it had already been in the media.

She did, however, attend a rally held by the Redstockings, one offshoot of the New York radicals, which claims coinage for phrases such as: "Sisterhood Is Powerful," "Consciousness Raising," and "The Politics of Housework." On March 21, they held a rally in Greenwich Village, which focused on abortion and women speaking out about their experiences. Because the crowd was standing room only, Gloria sat on a windowsill and listened to stories of women who had found themselves pregnant. "One woman's boyfriend had told her she couldn't get pregnant if it was his second orgasm. I can remember people laughing," she remarked.[4]

Many of the women were unlike Gloria in that they had risked the illegality and physical danger to obtain abortions, rather than following legal means, and some stories were sordid—stories about back alley practitioners causing infection, and the loss of fertility due to butchered procedures, stories of pain and suffering, and stories of other women's pain and death. Gloria related to these accounts because every one of the women who spoke or who were spoken about might have been her, and through these public admissions, she had an epiphany. Her bond with the women's movement was forged that night. Immediately, she knew that she *was* a feminist, and later wrote, "Suddenly, I was no longer learning intellectually what was wrong. I knew. I had had an abortion…why should each of us be made to feel criminal and alone?"[5]

This epiphany produced her first feminist article: "After Black Power, Women's Liberation" for her "City Politic" column in *New York* magazine, and it won the Penney-Missouri Journalism Award as one of the first stories to explain feminism.

At this time, Gloria was also writing some articles and a column for *Look* magazine (which ceased publication in 1971) and in hopes of gaining support for Cesar Chavez and La Causa, she interviewed him for *Look*. "The publisher turned it down because he was worried about losing ads from Sunkist (their oranges were picked by migrant workers), Pat [Carbine] was the one who intervened."[6] Patricia Carbine was the managing editor of *Look* at the time, and unbeknownst to Gloria, she told the publisher that if he did not publish Gloria's article, she would be forced to resign. Gloria would not know of this situation until many years later, but she always held high esteem for Carbine, with whom she would form a strong professional bond.

THE BRESLIN-MAILER CAMPAIGN

Gloria would also link with Norman Mailer and Jimmy Breslin, two writers who also produced articles for *New York* magazine. Although stories differ, *New York* editor Clay Felker said:

> One morning Peter Maas, Gloria Steinem, Jimmy Breslin, and I were sitting around in a restaurant around the corner from *New York* magazine and talking about the upcoming campaign. I don't remember the exact conversation, but it has been said by people who were there that I suggested that Breslin run for mayor and then write about it. Jimmy said, "No, no, no. We should get Mailer to run." So, when this took fire, I got Mailer and Breslin together in a photographer's studio, we shot a picture of the two of them, and used it as [*New York's*] cover picture. What we had was an inside track.[7]

Mailer had just been selected to win the Pulitzer prize for his *Armies of the Night: History as a Novel / The Novel as History,* which captured the 1967 antiwar march on the Pentagon via a nontraditional style. It was an early work of what has come to be known as creative nonfiction, carrying on the traditional nontradition of *New York* magazine's style into a book-length work. Breslin remarked that Mailer would have the best draw and agreed to run for city council president on the same ticket. They called their party the Left-Right Coalition, to promote the idea that both factions should have their say.

Yet, the campaign deteriorated into farce. The news media never took the Mailer-Breslin campaign seriously, and although they had strong ideas to present, neither man had the political mindset. According to Joe Mathewson in *Up Against Daley, The New Politics in Illinois*, "They ran a philosophical campaign based on a 'left-conservatism' platform of making New York [City] the 51st state and returning power to the neighborhoods."[8] They also advocated free bicycles in the parks, a Manhattan monorail and jitney service to provide access to the city after banning other motor traffic, and weekend jousting matches for teenagers. They wanted to get beyond the idea of management and present ideas that were nontraditional, to get to the heart of the people. Their slogan was "Vote the Rascals In."

During the campaign, Gloria was asked to run for comptroller. "[The thought] frightened me because I'd never spoken in public before."[9] However she never made the ticket, but the campaign lost impetus when Mailer appeared at a fund-raising dinner dead drunk and cursed obscenities at the audience. Gloria remarked, "I never considered it a serious effort in the sense they'd win, but I thought it was a creative way of inserting ideas into the campaign."[10] Throughout the process, she came to realize that Mailer held white men above all others, and his views made her uncomfortable.

MORE MIGRANT MARCHING

When Cesar Chavez called and asked Gloria to attain press coverage for the farmworkers' march from the California cities of Coachella to Calexico, she considered it a type of salvation from the campaign, although she still continued a long-distance participation. Gloria said, "Norman and I had dinner at one of those Aegean fish places, and I explained that I thought it was more important for me to be an outside organizer and press contact for the California farmworkers' march to the Mexican border. It was a fine, amicable conversation, and then I sort of just drifted away."[11]

As she prepared to go to California, Chavez organized the march on both sides of the border. Poor Mexican farm workers would meet American farm workers there and agree not to work against one another. Speeches would be made on the back of flatbed trucks, famous people would be invited to attend, and the ensuing celebration would bring publicity for La Causa. Senator Ted Kennedy came and future governor of California, Jerry Brown. Even some who were not supporters of the cause showed up, and Congressman John Tunney was booed for his lack of enthusiasm for the farmworkers' plight.

Gloria drove to Calexico with a United Farmworkers (UFW) lawyer and set up a communications center in a small motel there. From that phone, she called the press and many celebrities, asking them to attend. Chavez later wrote to Gloria, "[I am told] that you did a fantastic job of press relations."[12] Yet, Gloria was not a fan of Chavez, as he did not give recognition to the women helping the cause, such as Marion Moses and Delores Huerta. They had worked as hard or harder than Chavez himself, yet their contributions were rarely mentioned.

Still, Gloria sympathized with the farmworkers and lent support in any way she could. In fact, she ran up a rather large balance on her American Express card to cover all expenses of the trip and the press relations for the march, including the motel rooms, phone bills, and food. Ultimately, she did not have the money to repay the debt and the card was revoked. As this effort took so much time and energy away from her profession, Gloria backed away from full-time assistance, but continued to help in small ways, whenever she can.

NO BROADS ALLOWED

In July, Gloria shifted her focus to the national political scene when she received a phone call from Senator George McGovern. He asked her to attend a meeting, organized by Senator Abraham Ribicoff, to discuss McGovern's potential campaign for the presidency in 1972. McGovern asked Gloria to give thought to her advice before arriving. As Gloria had been out of the political arena for a while, she stopped to consider the situation in view of her recent feminist awakening.

Beforehand, she might have been flattered at the invitation to a male event, though she had done just as much or more than any of the male volunteers on the campaign. Her presence had been questioned during the last campaign, and she was even told not to appear conspicuous, lest voters get the wrong impression about her and McGovern having an affair. To minimize the effect, Gloria bought clothing that was more conservative in bland colors and tried to blend in with the walls, because it might be counterproductive for anyone to think that a *woman* had worked on speeches or had anything to do with policy.

And though she had brought in a $10,000 contribution from a single contributor, she was still treated like a frivolous woman, who should have no more inside her head than kitchen, kids, and church. She was not sure if she wanted to become involved in another male-oriented, male-dominated promotion. Then, she realized that her attendance at that meeting would be a blow against sexism and actually began to anticipate it with enthusiasm and wrote, "For one thing, I can finally stop couching my suggestions in hesitancy and humor."[13]

However, she would never attend that meeting. During a weekend in Vermont with the economist John Galbraith and his family the following month, McGovern explained to Gloria that Ribicoff had stricken her from the list of meeting attendees, and simply told McGovern, "No broads."[14] McGovern told Gloria that he had explained how the women had helped raise funds for the campaign, to write speeches, and helped with policy decisions in the last campaign. Yet, Ribicoff only listened and then repeated his statement. Gloria wondered if Ribicoff would have gotten away with such discrimination against blacks or Jews, while this prejudice against women attending an important political conference was perfectly acceptable. This situation made Gloria realize that nothing would change for women, unless women made it happen. She wondered whether women were up to the task, and in fact, wondered whether she herself had the strength and courage.

SPEAKING OUT

To test herself, Gloria forced herself to speak to groups about the status quo for women and why and how they could change it. Her first major speaking engagement was before the Women's National Democratic Club (WNDC), where she would discuss "After Civil Rights—Women's Liberation," and she was terrified. "I started out life as a writer, and writers write in part because they don't want to talk."[15] She considered offering the WNDC $1,000 to let her off the hook. Yet, shaking, she delivered her address.

After the speech, Barbara Howar, a renowned Washington personality and hostess, threw a party for Gloria, where she met up with Henry Kissinger, a Harvard professor at the time, serving as director of Harvard's Defense Studies Program and its International Seminar. Gloria had written a piece for New York soon after Richard Nixon's election in 1968, warning the people that Nixon had not changed, and to her surprise, Kissinger had called her to laud the work. They talked about the political atmosphere in Washington, and whether Kissinger would take a post with the Nixon administration, if offered. Kissinger brought up the advantages of working from the inside to make things better, and Gloria convinced him to write an article for New York, tentatively titled "The Collaboration Problem." He had covered this conundrum in his doctoral dissertation in regard to the relationship between Napoleon and Prince Klemens von Metternich. Metternich had been ambassador to Napoleon's court, representing the interests of his native Austria, a country for which Napoleon had a zest for conquering. Kissinger remarked, "To cooperate without losing one's soul, to assist without sacrificing one's identity, what harder test of moral toughness exists?"[16] The irony of the conversation was that Kissinger was tapped for a position in Nixon's cabinet within a few days.

When the two met at Howar's party, a photo was snapped of Kissinger and Gloria, which ran in the next day's *Washington Post,* and speculation about a relationship between the pair began. But though Gloria had had relationships with many celebrities—most recently Rafer Johnson, who had won the silver medal in the decathlon in the 1956 Olympics and the gold medal in 1960, and former Cleveland Brown and future pro Hall of Famer Jim Brown, she had no relationship with Kissinger and said so: "I am not nor have I ever been a girlfriend of Henry Kissinger's."[17] The photo that caused the media gossip had actually included George Mc-Govern, who had been strategically cropped out.

The year 1970 started with Gloria on the road, carrying the message of feminism to every group she could, but not alone. Speaking before large groups still terrified her, and so, Dorothy Pitman Hughes, an African American who ran a child care center in New York's Upper West Side, agreed to speak with her. Hughes was at ease speaking to people, as she had several years' civil rights experience, and Gloria felt that she would be helpful in paralleling the plight of women with that of the discrimination against people of color. Their first engagement was at New York University, but soon the two were flying to all parts of America.

In any engagement, Gloria always spoke first because she felt that anything she had to say would be a dénouement to what her partner said. Even Gloria admitted that she was dependent on the approval of others, making the task of public speaking no less agonizing as time went on. Yet, she was able to touch people with her charm and unassuming ways. She remembers being tapped on the shoulder by a gray-haired woman with gnarled hands in Detroit, who told her, "I just want you to know you are the inside of me."[18]

The message of feminism was spreading throughout the world. Women realized that they wanted equality and were determined to get it. On March 16, 1970, 46 researchers at *Newsweek* magazine filed formal charges of discrimination and on March 18, more than 100 women from 10 different groups stormed the offices of the *Ladies Home Journal* and staged an 11-hour sit-in, protesting the image of women portrayed in the magazine and the status of the women employed there.

CONTROVERSY WITHIN

Yet, there were rifts in the movement. Controversy came from Betty Friedan's speech at the third annual NOW convention on March 20, when she retired after four years, the organization's constitutional limit. In the two hour discourse, she called for a Women's Strike for Equality, urged all American women to join, and proposed the date to be August 26, the 50th anniversary of the 19th Amendment, which gave women the right to vote. With this statement, she floored the new NOW leadership; the announcement had taken them completely by surprise. Apparently, Friedan did not plan to fade away, and her announcement had NOW in an uproar.

Other dissentions brewing threatened to shatter the movement, and it also began with NOW. When writer Rita Mae Brown joined the group, she introduced herself as the "token lesbian" in the room.[19] At the time, alternate lifestyles were not acceptable to American society, and to admit homosexuality was a major decision that could affect a person's entire life. People were fired for being gay, ridiculed, and even physically abused. Gay women had begun to distrust the leaders of the movement, feeling that they were being shunned for the sake of appearances. Yet, they did not want the movement to be about their sexuality or anyone else's. The movement was about equality for all, and as religious beliefs had no bearing, neither should sexual orientation. Carol Schmidt, a feminist and a lesbian, wrote:

> I dropped out of feminism until I was safely married (to a man) a few years later and could reemerge with that protective wedding ring as I entered the L.A. Women's Center on Crenshaw for the next phase of my activism. Just as the tactics adapted from Gandhi for the civil rights movement transferred easily to the antiwar movement, now we used the same experiences for feminism.
>
> The marriage didn't last long. Neither did my straight facade. The day [my husband] left me, I attended a women's conference at Santa Monica Community College and fell in lust with 200 women. Suddenly all the hidden issues of lesbian-straight conflicts in the movement were right in my face. And Gloria Steinem, the beautiful straight woman who was so tal-

ented and who didn't even seem to have a flaw, was a focal
point for those conflicts. I loved her and hated her. Many of us
did.[20]

Still Betty Friedan, with her statements and behaviors toward gay
women, was the main target. Susan Brownmiller, an author and early
member of the New York Radical Feminists, wrote, "Friedan was apoplec-
tic. A survivor of the fifties, when union people and progressives were red-
baited and hounded, she had a premonition that the same thing would
happen to the women's movement, with dyke baiting as the inquisitors'
tactic. Friedan took stock of the loose cannon and started muttering about
the Lavender Menace."[21]

After a few months, Brown asked why NOW never raised lesbian issues
at their meetings. When her question was answered by a stony silence, it
was evident that lesbians were not welcome in the organization, and
Brown resigned her membership. In the New York NOW newsletter, she
wrote, "Lesbianism is the one word which gives the New York NOW executive committee a collective heart attack,"[22] and shifted to the Redstockings, who were more accepting of people with alternate lifestyles.
Other lesbian feminist organizations were the Daughters of Bilitis, the
Gay Liberation Front, and the soon to be Radicalesbians, organized by
Brown herself.

Not meaning to make matters worse, Brownmiller wrote an article for
New York Times Magazine, entitled "Sisterhood is Powerful: A Member of
the Women's Liberation Movement Explains What It's All About," in
which she commented on the "Lavender Menace" epithet, remarking
that it was not a menace at all, but a lavender herring, and that lesbians
were certainly no imminent danger to the movement. Although Brownmiller meant this to be a humorous remark, the lesbian feminists did not
take it as such and went into planning a major demonstration. Feminist
Karla Jay wrote, "Susan's detractors believed that her comments were
even worse than Betty's: They were a dismissal of lesbians as totally unim-
portant, an unnecessary distraction from the real issue."[23]

On May 1, at the Second Congress to Unite Women, the lesbian faction staged the Lavender Menace Action with the hope that it would spur
heterosexual feminists to acknowledge lesbian wants and needs, along
with their own. About 40 women came in wearing pink T-shirts with the
words "Lavender Menace" printed on the front and carrying placards,
reading such things as: "Take a Lesbian to Lunch" and "We Are Your
Worst Nightmare." After a staged surprise, where pink shirted women
lined each aisle, holding placards and inviting others to join them from

the audience, the group passed out their "The Woman-Identified Woman" manifesto, and the event marked the relationship of the two groups from that point forward.

PUSHING THE ERA

Also in the first week of May, Gloria testified before a Senate Subcommittee on the Equal Rights Amendment (ERA). In her speech, she argued that opposition to the ERA was founded in erroneous thinking about gender differences and that these biased sentiments were promoted by white male domination. "The truth is that all our problems stem from the same sex based myths. We may appear before you as white radicals or the middle-aged middle class or black soul sisters, but we are all sisters in fighting against these outdated myths. Like racial myths, they have been reflected in our laws."[24] She then went on to address myths that women were biologically inferior, that women were already being treated equally in society, that American women held great economic power, that children required full-time mothers, and that the women's movement was not political or serious.

Before and after her testimony, Gloria continued her missionary role. Dorothy Pitman Hughes had dropped out of speaking with her, as she had a baby and decided to stop traveling, and lawyer and feminist activist Florynce (Flo) Kennedy joined her instead. Kennedy was flamboyant and energized crowds. She once said, "There are very few jobs that actually require a penis or a vagina."[25] Kennedy also had a good relationship with the Black Panthers, the militant black civil rights group, and the two women attracted a broad-based audience.

In June, Gloria spoke alone at the commencement at Vassar. She said, "The important thing is that we are spending this time together, considering the larger implications of a movement that some call 'feminist' but should more accurately be called humanist; a movement that is an integral part of rescuing this country from its old, expensive patterns of elitism, racism, and violence."[26] She went on to discuss how students were taught white men's history and stressed the need for women's studies and black studies courses in American colleges. She paralleled the two causes, saying that Americans had been taught to believe that women and blacks were somehow inferior, but pointed out that women with college degrees, working full-time, still made less than black men, who made less than white men. She also pointed out how unfairly women were treated under the law, saying that married women had no legal right to own property as single entities until the mid-nineteenth century or even to be served in a restaurant and that she could be denied service based solely on the basis of her gender. She pointed out that children would benefit by having the attention of both parents, not just that of a full-time mother, and that women are entitled to have private identities, to be who and what they wanted to be. "The point is that Women's Liberation is not destroying the American family; it is trying to build a human, compassionate alternative out of its ruins."[27]

THE RADICAL CHIC

Gloria's nontraditional ideas brought her admiration from women around the country, which translated into dollars for the movement. However, when Tom Wolfe wrote his jabbing "Radical Chic, That Party at Lenny's" article in *New York* magazine about symphony conductor Leonard Bernstein's party for the Black Panthers, her contributors hesitated. Wolfe wrote:

> That huge Panther there, the one Felicia is smiling her tango smile at, is Robert Bay, who just 41 hours ago was arrested in an altercation with the police, supposedly over a .38-caliber revolver that someone had, in a parked car in Queens at Northern Boulevard and 104th Street or some such unbelievable place, and taken to jail on a most unusual charge called "criminal facilitation." And now he is out on bail and walking into Leonard and Felicia Bernstein's 13-room penthouse duplex on Park Avenue. Harrassment & Hassles, Guns & Pigs, Jail & Bail—they're real, these Black Panthers.[28]

He then went on to list guests, alluding to the fact that the rich jet-setters could otherwise never have had contact with the fashionable cause they were backing. The people Wolfe roasted did not mind giving to organizations they sympathized with, but not at the expense of ridicule, and for a while, people were hesitant to donate to feminism or any other cause regardless of its worth.

Yet, efforts throughout the women's movement continued. After retiring from NOW, Betty Friedan took to planning a fund-raising party for her Women's Strike Coalition and invited such luminaries as heiress and fashion designer Gloria Vanderbilt and Gloria Steinem to be on the coordinating committee. The event took place on August 9, 1970 at the Scull estate in the Hamptons of New York. The pastoral setting of manicured gardens and green spans of grass, with tasteful sculptures placed throughout the landscape, gave the gathering an air of class and distinction. During her rally speech, Friedan stood at a microphone, urging people to donate to the Women's Strike for Equality, and denigrated Tom Wolfe's radical chic image. She intoned, "It is time to finish the unfinished revolution of American women.... This party is a great event...a political event and not just a fashionable event to get women into the paper!"[29]

Suddenly, Jill Johnston, a columnist for *The Village Voice*, stripped off her jeans and jumped into the swimming pool. As she rose to the surface, she whipped off her shirt and in only her underpants, floated on her back. Friedan was furious and muttered about the woman, "One of the biggest enemies of this movement..."[30] And with that comment, the top of Friedan's low-cut dress fell down from the weight of a political button, exposing most of one breast. Though the party made money, the public relations for the movement was devastating, as the surprise events made comical fodder for the New York press.

STRIKE FOR EQUALITY

On August 20, New York NOW members organized a demonstration at the Statue of Liberty. They had ferried across to Liberty Island with huge banners in sections and hung them across the railing before the statue, which read: "WOMEN OF THE WORLD UNITE" and "STRIKE AUGUST 26."

On the morning of the march, Friedan told reporters, "This is our hour of history. We're going to take it."[31] The protest would wind down Fifth Avenue to Bryant Park, where Gloria would emcee a host of other celebrities, including Congresswomen Shirley Chisholm and Bella Abzug, comedienne Joan Rivers, Flo Kennedy, and rising feminists Kate Millet and Ti-Grace Atkinson, who would speak to the crowd. Just before the march, Friedan was handed a proclamation from the deputy mayor, declaring Women's Equality Day in New York. Soon, thousands of men and women, including members of NOW, YWCA, the Redstockings, New York Radical Feminists, and Radicalesbians amassed and marched toward the park, with Gloria and Friedan at the lead. Gloria carried a placard, showing the recently disclosed My Lai massacre in Vietnam, bearing the words: "Q:...and children? A:...and children. The Masculine Mystique."[32]

Along the route, hecklers cried out to the marching feminists: "Baby killers!" and other debasing expletives. Yet, other feminists, who could not join the march for personal reasons, were also lining their path, cheering them on. The gathering went well, and Gloria excelled in her master of ceremonies duty so well that other groups would constantly demand her for this role in the future.

Demonstrations took place in cities all over the country that day and it became evident that people were beginning to take the movement seriously. New York Governor Nelson Rockefeller proclaimed August 26 Women's Rights Day in New York. President Nixon issued a proclamation assuring women of a wider role in society. This new credibility gave women in the movement more power. They could now campaign seriously for women's rights in every corner of the world.

BACKLASH

However, the media was fueling petty fires. In the week of the Strike for Equality, *Time* magazine published an article about Kate Millet and in an artist's rendering, splashed her face across the cover, declaring her the "Mao Tse-tung of Women's Liberation."[33] Millet was aghast! She had told the reporter that if they were writing about the movement and not just her new book *Sexual Politics*, that Betty Friedan should be on the cover. Although she had been assured that they wanted to get everyone involved, the magazine portrayed her as a significant driving force of the movement, when she was only the education director of New York NOW. Yet, she was and would continue to be an ardent feminist.

In October, she was scheduled to discuss the women's movement at Columbia University and found herself before a hostile audience. After her speech, there were questions from the floor: "Are you a lesbian?"[34] Millet was married and in reality thought of herself as bisexual, but had never made the fact public. Then, the question was repeated: "Are you a lesbian? Say it!"[35] To that, Millet finally replied, "Yes, I am a lesbian."[36]

Millet knew the NOW stance on lesbians in the feminist community. It certainly had not been encouraged by Friedan, and Susan Brownmiller thought the issue of homosexuality was counterproductive to the cause. They did not want those outside the movement to see them as a crowd of dykes and lezzies. Sexuality was not the issue: discrimination against women, regardless of race, creed, or sexual preference was.

The morning following the Columbia outing of Millet, a *Time* magazine reporter showed up on Millet's doorstep and asked whether she had actually said she was a lesbian. Not realizing to whom she was talking, Millet said, "Yes."[37] The result was a December 14 issue of *Time*, offering a second look at women's lib, a negative commentary on feminists, which used Millet's sexuality to bludgeon the movement.

Ivy Bottini, president of New York NOW, said, "This is the real test of sisterhood. We've got to stand behind Kate."[38] At another Women's Strike Coalition march on December 12, originally intended as a march in support of child care centers and abortion, Millet's outing came to the forefront as a freedom of choice issue. Lavender armbands began to show up on the participants, and leaflets were passed out explaining their meaning. "It's not one woman's sexual experience that is under attack," the pamphlet said. "It is the freedom of all women to openly state values that fundamentally challenge the basic structure of patriarchy.... SISTERHOOD *IS* POWERFUL!!!"[39]

When Friedan was handed an armband, she briefly looked at the piece of light purple cloth and then allowed it to fall to the floor. She later wrote:

> The Women's Strike Coalition was planning to hold a press conference, they told me, and declare we were all lesbians, in solidarity with Kate and other bisexuals and lesbians, struggling for liberation in a sexist society. I was vehemently opposed and told them so. I was certainly in solidarity with Kate and with the other friends of mine in the movement who happened to be lesbians. And I was and am against repression of any kind. But I didn't think it was a good strategic tactic in any way. To say, 'We are all lesbians,' was total bullshit, and I wasn't going to do it.[40]

At the time, others held that Friedan was unhappy that the effort had been planned without her participation.

On December 18, the Kate Is Great press conference was held. Sitting at a table with about 50 supporters behind her and Gloria beside her holding her hand, Millet said, "Women's liberation and homosexual liberation are both struggling towards a common goal: a society free from defining and categorizing people by virtue of gender and/or sexual preference."[41] With such well-known and respected women as Gloria, Flo Kennedy, Susan Brownmiller, Ivy Bottini, and Ti-Grace Atkinson, Millet maintained that "Women's autonomy is what women's liberation is all about."[42]

To that end, the women needed a newsletter, something to spread the word that women's liberation was not about sexuality, it was about humanism. For Gloria, another cause within the cause was about to begin.

NOTES

1. Quoted in Ellen Messer-Davidow, "Feminist Theory and Criticism, 1. 1963–1972," in *The Johns Hopkins Guide to Literary Theory and Criticism*, edited by Michael Groden and Martin Kreiswirth, 1997, http://www.press.jhu.edu/books/hopkins_guide_to_literary_theory/feminist_theory_and_criticism-1.html.

2. Ibid.

3. Steinem, *Revolution from Within*, p. 23.

4. Susan Dominus, "30th Anniversary Issue/Gloria Steinem: First Feminist," *New York*, 6 April 1998, http://www.newyorkmetro.com/mynetro/news/people/features/2438/index.html.

5. Steinem, *Outrageous Acts*, p. 20.

6. Steinem, *Moving Beyond Words*, p. 134.

7. Quoted in Peter Manso, *Mailer, His Life and Times* (New York: Simon and Schuster, 1985), p. 498.

8. Quoted in Dick Simpson and George Beam, *Strategies for Change: How to Make the American Political Dream Work* (Chicago: Swallow Press, 1976), p. 237.

9. Quoted in Manso, *Mailer*, p. 501.

10. Ibid., pp. 501–2.

11. Ibid., p. 503.

12. Quoted in Heilbrun, *Education of a Woman*, p. 157.

13. Steinem, *Outrageous Acts*, p. 115.

14. Ibid., p. 116.

15. Dominus, "30th Anniversary."

16. Quoted in Walter Isaacson, *Kissinger* (New York: Simon and Schuster, 1992), p. 134.

17. Ibid., p. 356.

18. Steinem, *Outrageous Acts*, p. 30.

19. Brownmiller, *In Our Time*, p. 71.

20. Carol Schmidt, interview with author, 23 March 2003.

21. Brownmiller, *In Our Time*, p. 71.

22. Quoted in Flora Davis, *Moving the Mountain* (New York: Simon and Schuster, 1991), p. 263.

23. Jay, *Memoir of Liberation*, p. 140.

24. Senate Committee on the Judiciary, *The "Equal Rights" Amendment: Hearings before the Subcommittee on Constitutional Amendments of the Committee on the Judiciary*, 91st Cong., 2nd sess., 5–7 May 1970.

25. Quoted in Cohen, *The Sisterhood*, p. 162.

26. Gloria Steinem, "Living the Revolution," 1970, *The Alumni Quarterly* (Vassar College), http://www.aavc.vassar.edu/vq/spring2002/extras/steinem.html.

27. Steinem, "Living the Revolution."

28. Tom Wolfe, *Radical Chic and Mau-Mauing the Flak Catchers* (New York: Farrar, Straus & Giroux, 1970; reprint, New York: Bantam, 1983), p. 4 (page citation is to reprint edition).

29. Quoted in Cohen, *The Sisterhood*, p. 277.

30. Ibid., p. 278

31. Ibid., p. 281

32. Ibid., p. 277.

33. Quoted in Stern, *Gloria Steinem*, p. 217.

34. Quoted in Cohen, *The Sisterhood*, p. 243

35. Ibid.

36. Ibid.

37. Ibid., p. 244.

38. Ibid., p. 248.

39. Ibid., p. 249.

40. Betty Friedan, *Life So Far, a Memoir* (New York: Simon and Schuster, 2000), p. 249.

41. Quoted in Cohen, *The Sisterhood*, p. 251.

42. Ibid.

Chapter 10

A GRUELING LIFE

Gloria came to the forefront of American pop culture in 1971. *Vogue*, *Redbook, Esquire,* and McCall's magazines all did profiles of her. Although she continued to travel and speak to feminist groups around the country, a new project was on the horizon—one that would frustrate her, overburden her, and become the crowning achievement of her life. That year, Gloria would also find that the price of fame is often higher than expected.

In November of 1970, Brenda Feigen, the national vice president for legislation of NOW and a Harvard Law graduate, began discussing a new politically oriented organization for women. She had seen Gloria on the David Susskind talk show in 1969 and was so impressed that she had recruited Gloria for her testimony before the Senate subcommittee and worked closely with her toward ratification of the ERA. The two were perfect allies. Whereas Feigen was outspoken and confident, Gloria was subdued and reticent to involve herself in direct conflict. Feigen intended to bring Gloria into her plans.

Feigen had come to see that NOW was not capable of dealing with grassroots problems and saw the need for a new association, which she, Gloria, and others would found and call the Women's Action Alliance (WAA). It would address relief from everyday problems women suffered, such as gender discrimination in the workplace, sexual harassment, spousal abuse, and the alteration or eradication of sexist textbooks. Their initial press release of January 12, 1972, read: "We are announcing today the formation of the Women's Action Alliance, a tax-exempt organization designed to assist women working on practical, local action projects; projects that attack the special problems of social dependence, discrimination, and limited life alternatives they face because they are women."[1]

Gloria and Feigen felt so strongly about the need for the WAA that they worked throughout 1971 to establish the organization. When the announcement of its inception was made, mail from abused and snubbed women poured in by the sackful to their office on Lexington Avenue. The incredible response prompted Gloria to see the need for a newsletter. The purpose was twofold—to keep readers informed and to provide income for the organization. The opening gatherings regarding the newsletter included writer Jane O'Reilly; Congresswoman Bella Abzug; Dorothy Pitman Hughes; Floryence Kennedy; Shirley Kalunda, the lone African American advertising executive at J. Walter Thompson; and ex-Beatle John Lennon and his wife Yoko Ono.

Yet, Feigen told Gloria they should forget the newsletter and go straight to a glossy, color magazine. However, according to *Inside Ms., 25 Years of the Magazine and the Feminist Movement*, Patricia Carbine, former editor of *Look* and new editor of *McCall's*, was the determining factor. Carbine said, "If what you're really trying to do is create a forum, a place where women could talk to each other, it's got to be in a magazine format."[2] Discussions over this idea and what format the publication would take continued for several months.

GLORIA THE MISSIONARY

In the meantime, Gloria was becoming recognized by sight and reputation. Her long, straight blond hair, parted in the middle, framed her pretty face, which sported tinted aviator-style glasses, placed over sections of her hair rather than underneath. Her elegance and style of dress was diametrically opposed to many people's vision of a stereotypical feminist. Gloria showed that not all feminists were homely, overweight, homosexual, or sexually repressed, as the movement's detractors painted everyone in the group to be. Gloria became an icon of feminism, a beautiful package, delivering a potent message with a quirky sense of humor. Not everyone loved her, but everyone was certainly intrigued.

During 1971, Gloria also continued speaking and was the first woman to be invited to address the Harvard Law Review banquet. At first, Gloria was intimidated by the guests who would be on hand. Past and present members of the Harvard Law Review staff would attend and of course, all of them would be men, as none of the reporters or editors had ever been female. As lawyers, they would certainly all be critical, and Gloria turned the invitation down. Yet, women law students insisted that Gloria accept and speak about discriminatory practices at Harvard. And she did.

Her opening remarks were that she had wanted to go to law school after graduating Smith—Phi Beta Kappa—but was discouraged. Both Harvard and Columbia law schools had admitted some women, but they were considered outsiders, and she felt it was time to set Harvard straight. Feminism was the only route to humanism, and Gloria declared that it was a path toward which Harvard Law School showed no impetus. She mentioned that Harvard had no classes about or for women, including nothing on the ERA or anything showing that women lost many civil rights upon marrying.

When Steinem completed her speech, delineating very specific instances where Harvard Law could improve its stance on women, an angry professor rose and attempted a rebuttal. Yet, he was so unprepared and so hysterical over what Gloria had said that his loose speech fell apart and the gentleman embarrassed himself. In the history of the banquet, Gloria's speech was the first requiring this perceived necessity for rebuttal; however, what Gloria had projected was correct. Even the administration came to see that their stance toward women had to be corrected, and changes began to occur.

This ability to staunchly defend her beliefs is important to who Gloria is as a person. Although she felt timid about speaking in front of people, once she began, there would be no stopping her. This strength and conviction, her wit, and her intelligence showed through, and Gloria had proved to the world that she was not just another pretty face, but a force to affect change in the nation. Her message could not be denied.

This strength of character continued to attract influential and powerful men. During the first months of 1971, she became involved with Franklin Thomas, who would later become the President of the Ford Foundation. At the time he dated Gloria seriously, he was president and CEO of the Bedford-Stuyvesant Restoration Corporation, which aimed to redevelop the Bedford-Stuyvesant community in Brooklyn, New York. They met through a panel discussion where they discussed Brooklyn College's urban justice issues. Thomas was African American and known for hiring women into nontraditional positions, such as those of construction worker or community leader. Gloria saw black men as more understanding of women's anger over stereotyping, as they had so often been stereotyped themselves. Gloria's relationship with Thomas lasted three years and ended when they realized how much they were alike. They decided they would be better off remaining friends.

A FIRST POLITICAL FIRING

This symbiosis between sexism and racism was shown to include black women in a Louis Harris poll reported near the end of May. The poll showed that 42 percent of all women favored efforts to change their status in society, while 43 percent opposed. Yet, among black women, 62 percent approved of feminist efforts, while only 20 percent opposed. In 1971, black women were still the most repressed people in America. They dealt with both racism and sexism at once, and many were infuriated by the status quo.

Angela Davis was one of these women. She became a member of the Communist Party and the Black Panthers, while earning her master's degree from the University of California at San Diego. She obtained an assistant professorship at the University of California at Los Angeles; however, after one year's employment, she was dismissed by the university for her radical connections. Also because of the groups she associated with, she was watched closely by the United States government and in the fall of 1970, was added to the FBI's most wanted list. She was charged with being an accessory to a violent shootout during a jailbreak for one of the Soledad Brothers, who were accused of killing a guard at the Soledad prison in California. She was subsequently acquitted, but spent 16 months in jail before she was set free.

Believing that Davis was wrongly accused and only suffering harassment at the hands of the government for her political views and associations, Gloria became Treasurer of the Committee for the Legal Defense of Angela Davis, which cost her a $5,000 per year contract to consult for *Seventeen* magazine. Viewing the event as her first firing for political reasons, the loss did not affect her significantly.

JABS FROM WITHIN

One issue that would continue to affect Gloria for years would be the tension between her and Betty Friedan. Friedan saw herself as the seminal influence that began the women's movement, and once remarked, "I wouldn't say that I started the movement; it surely is a product of historical forces, but if Betty Friedan weren't alive, she'd have to be invented to see the movement through."[3] But when Friedan and Gloria stood side by side, Gloria was the preferred photo subject. She was beautiful and elegant, whereas Betty was average and short, and the media always tend to promote the photogenic.

Partially because of this, Betty developed a strong dislike of Gloria. This was true, although Betty and Gloria had much in common. Obviously, they were both committed to the women's movement, both were graduates of Smith College, both had Jewish heritage, and both were journalists. Yet, they could not be friends. Betty used Gloria at the party in the Hamptons as hostess when she perceived no threat, but when Betty began to think that Gloria would take the movement from her, she became Gloria's enemy and called her The Hair behind her back.

Gloria ignored the slights and went on to promote the idea of a new publication. In April, a prospectus appeared, entitled "Some notes on a new magazine..."[4] and it was marked "Confidential."[5] Gloria was stipulated as editor at large, with the publisher as Elizabeth (Betty) Forsling Harris. Harris had been publishing a women's newsletter in California and had been recommended to Brenda Feigen by a political acquaintance as someone who knew how to raise money. The booklet also specified "The editor of a leading national magazine will join the magazine as editor."[6] The sentence referred to Pat Carbine, who had decided to leave her new position at *McCall's* to work for the new magazine. Betty Friedan was not included in any of the discussions, and was not given any part in the new magazine.

Friedan was also devastated to learn that Gloria had been chosen to deliver the Smith commencement address in the spring of 1971. Friedan biographer Judith Hennessee commented, "That was a slap in the face, as if to her own family had adopted an orphan and loved it more than they loved her. Actually, the senior class, not the administration, had chosen Gloria, and she had not been their first choice, but that was no consolation."[7] Betty saw herself as the ugly stepsister, and as she had been the ignition for the women's movement, she was furious.

Gloria brought up the issue of image in her address to the Smith graduates. "Beautiful women have their own kind of problem. It's a kind of you-get-the-liquor-we'll-get-the-girls psychology, which means that women are interchangeable moving parts; that a beautiful woman is much less likely to be taken seriously as a human being than a less attractive one. And the unattractive ones have fundamentally the same problem because all that they are, all that they try to do, is written off with the argument, 'Well, they are only doing it because they can't get a man.' So-called beautiful and so-called ugly women have a common cause and should not be divided from each other."[8]

Gloria did not show the same animosity for Friedan, perhaps because she was the pretty one or perhaps because she never intended for people

to think that she was the initiator of the feminist movement. She remarked, "As a writer, I think I can sometimes provide language that al-
lows people to come together around common dreams. As a speaker, I can
make a space where people can talk to each other."[9] She prefers to be
thought of as an "organizer." "I don't want the power to dictate; at most,
only to persuade or inspire by raising our sights of what is possible."[10]
However, Gloria would continue to be disliked and slighted by Friedan.

THE BIRTH OF *MS.*

In July, the arrangement to publish the new women's magazine was finalized when Gloria, Harris, and Carbine each contributed $126.67 for
stock in Majority Enterprises. They had tentatively entitled the publishing venture *Everywoman*, but *Sisters, Lilith,* and *Sojourner* were also considered as titles for the new magazine. The term "Ms." was new, and still
not used by public institutions. Although a "Sisters" had been preferred by
a strong contingent, Gloria stuck to her opinion that *Ms.* was precisely
the title they needed, a symbolic word that enveloped the movement.
Women no longer wanted to be defined by marital status, and the term
was non-traditional, precisely what Gloria wanted the magazine to be.

But the novelty of the magazine's title did not help the founders to attain the funds needed to publish. Betty Harris had raised $5,000 by selling
some Majority Enterprises stock to a friend in California, but that was all
they had, and she had used some of it to set up a small office on Lexington
Avenue and 41st Street. So, in October, Gloria visited an old acquaintance she had made at Barbara Howar's party in 1969—Katherine Graham of the *Washington Post*. Gloria had spoken to her on other occasions
about the feminist movement, although Graham was not convinced. Graham wrote:

> I was pretty certain that whatever authentic self I may have
> had had been pretty well squelched, but Gloria kept telling me
> that if I came to understand what the women's movement was
> all about it would make my life much better. In time it in-
> evitably dawned on me, and how right she was! Later, when
> Gloria came to me for fund to start up Ms. magazine, I put up
> $20,000 for seed money to help her get going.[11]

Soon after that, in August 1971, Clay Felker agreed to finance a sam-
ple issue of the new magazine. He would publish a large portion of it in the

year-end double issue of *New York,* and then as a one-shot preview publication, it would hit the stands bearing its own logo. The profits would be split equally and Felker would have no future interest in the magazine. Gloria immediately set to deciding the content for the first issue and assigned articles to various writers.

THE NATIONAL WOMEN'S POLITICAL CAUCUS

After the Women's Strike for Equality, it became obvious that women needed a political alliance, an organization that would increase the number of women in politics and increase awareness of women's issues. Betty Friedan avers that the idea was hers, as she had begun speaking publicly about such an alliance in early 1971, while her opponents saw Bella Abzug as the creator of the new organization—the National Women's Political Caucus (NWPC). Gloria said, "My emotional memory is that it was not Betty's or any single person's idea. It was a spontaneous feeling that there needed to be women in the system and an organization devoted to electing them that would support women's issues. At that point, NOW was not doing it and did not want to. People said, as long as Betty is involved it won't happen."[12] Friedan just seemed to rub too many people the wrong way. Yet, Friedan says that she and Abzug began the organization simultaneously.

Actually, several women played key roles in development of this organization, including Friedan, Abzug, Gloria, and Shirley Chisholm, the first African American woman elected to Congress; Hawaiian Congresswoman Patsy Mink; Liz Carpenter, whom Abzug objected to, since she was former press secretary to Lady Bird Johnson; vice president of the National Welfare Rights Organization, Beulah Sanders; and Edith Van Horn, the first woman to serve on the executive board of the United Auto Workers. Their first meeting took place on June 9, 1971, in Abzug's congressional office, with Friedan, Abzug, Chisholm, and Gloria at the lead. Quickly, they found that their ideas about which candidates they would promote differed. Friedan wanted to support women candidates, regardless of their views, while Gloria, Chisholm, and Abzug insisted that they help only those dedicated to social improvement. And though the latter group wanted to take time to organize before gathering the troops, Friedan wanted the caucus to have impact at the 1972 Democratic presidential convention and set off to get the ball rolling.

Though Gloria had been intimidated by the outspoken and bold Abzug at first, they had become friends when Gloria worked on her 1970 political campaign. Gloria, of course, allied herself with the Abzug camp, but not because the two women had become friendly. It was because they were of like minds when it came to politics and Gloria knew that Abzug was a fair match for Friedan, while Gloria abhorred confrontation.

At the organizing conference, which took place between July 10 and 11 at the Statler Hilton Hotel in Washington, D.C., 2,000 women from all races, creeds, generations, sexual orientations, and positions gathered. And while they vied for leadership of the caucus, Friedan and Abzug fought over strategy, structure, and governing of the assembly. They were both forceful and unpredictable, and a leader with a leveler head was required, if they wanted to be taken seriously. And then, there was Gloria—Gloria, who packed a quiet wallop in a velvet fist. Because Friedan wanted to be the spokesperson so badly, Gloria believed it precipitated later attacks. Regarding Friedan's animosity over assuming the role of spokesperson for the organizers, Gloria said, "She never forgave me for that."[13]

A statement of purpose was presented, but no one really knew who was behind it. Letty Cotton Pogrebin had been called by Friedan to the conference to help with organization. She had recently begun a column in the *Ladies Home Journal*, entitled "Working Women," and like Gloria, had begun speaking about the women's movement. She had been an important publicist and publishing executive in New York and had also written the book *How to Make It in a Man's World*. Of the statement of purpose she said, "People never knew Gloria was the author of it. It had no authorship. She just put out and did it. I said to myself that I want to work with this woman. I want to be part of whatever she's part of."[14] Unknowingly, Gloria had made an important contact and a lifelong friend.

On August 16, Gloria hit the cover of *Newsweek* just a few days before the second New York City march of the Women's Strike Coalition. It was a glowing profile of an angry and elegant Phi Beta Kappa, extolling Gloria's strengths and ignoring her weaknesses. The article implied that she could have whatever she wanted without dedicating herself to such a challenging cause. Friedan even managed a compliment, "The fact that Gloria is very pretty and chic is nice for the movement, but if that's all she was it wouldn't be enough. Fortunately, she is so much more."[15]

BAD PRESS AND ULTIMATE SUCCESS

However, along with Friedan, not everyone had jumped on the I Love Gloria bandwagon. In October, *Esquire* magazine printed a negative profile of Gloria, entitled "She, The Awesome Power of Gloria Steinem." In the story, author Leonard Levitt reduced Gloria's accomplishments by describing her relationships with men as opportunistic and referred to her as "the intellectuals' pinup."[16] The article also disclosed that Gloria had been misstating her age by two years. In just a few thousand words, her acumen in the political arena had been blown away like a puff of smoke. Her career of crafting interesting words as a writer, which had earned her plum assignments from men and women editors alike, had been likened to payment for the mere hint of sexual attention. And there was nothing she could do.

Underlying this attack was the fear men had of being overpowered by women, of losing their masculinity, in other words—control. As a beautiful woman, Gloria could hold power over any man, without any kind of agenda. The fact that she wanted equal rights for her gender while using this sexual power was something that men did not want to consider. What would happen if all attractive women wanted important power too— power in the boardrooms, power in politics, and power in economics? At the time, men were not sure what their role might be in a world run by women. Gloria, and all other intelligent, beautiful women like her were perceived as a threat by many men, though that had never been Gloria's intention. The movement was not about taking over; it was about being equal, and men just did not get it.

Gloria continued her speaking engagements while fighting this nasty backlash and fulfilling her duties as editor at Ms. Yet, she had to change speaking partners once again. Still wanting racial balance, she chose another African American activist, Margaret Sloan, also a lesbian. Sloan had been introduced to Gloria by Flo Kennedy and had met her in Chicago where Sloan fought for civil rights. Kennedy wanted to bow out, as she had a busy schedule of organizing and writing, along with various health problems. Gloria had built a relationship with Sloan when she encouraged her to write for Ms. Another positive aspect of the Steinem-Sloan partnership was that Sloan agreed to be bodyguard and extricate Gloria from the throngs that now wanted to have her attention.

In the last week of December the premiere issue of Ms. hit the newsstands with 300,000 copies dated spring, 1972 and were trucked cross-country for distribution with Gloria doing the national public relations, along with the Ms. writers. Due to their efforts and the quality and content of the magazine, 26,000 subscriptions were garnered and more than 20,000 readers wrote letters in response. Even more encouraging was that the magazine completely sold out in only eight days.

Yet, not all was going well back in the Ms. offices. Felker and Harris were not getting along, and Harris was severely disgusted that Gloria had become the focus of attention over the success of Ms.; since Harris was the publisher; she thought she deserved the media attention. At the office, she was harsh with the staff. Gloria and Carbine lost patience with Harris. The contract for Majority Enterprises stipulated that if any one of the three partners were to leave the magazine, they would sell their stock back to the corporation for a reasonable fee. Although Harris tried to raise the funds to take over Ms. on her own, she was unsuccessful and eventually settled for $36,000, representing all proceeds from the premiere issue, and retained one-third of her stock, or about 10 percent of the company. She was also to be paid $2,000 per month and her name would stay on the masthead of the magazine as cofounder for 14 months.

The year 1972 was involved not only with the machinations at Ms., but also with politics. Shirley Chisholm announced her candidacy for president of the United States in January of 1972, providing Gloria with a conundrum, since she had previously backed George McGovern. She also wanted to back Shirley as the first black woman to run for president.

The ERA was still on Gloria's mind as well. The controversy rose when the amendment passed in the Senate on March 22, with a vote of 84 to 8, and it was sent to the 50 states for ratification. Backlash from anti-ERA activists, such as ultraconservative Phyllis Schlafly, a St. Louis lawyer, and her Eagle Forum rose to block the legislation and saw major obstacles on such issues as: making women equally responsible for support of the family as men are today, thus undermining the family; requiring 18-year-old women to register for the military draft; and refuting a wife's right to half of her husband's social security benefits after his death.

These anti-ERA proponents also saw the ERA not as a bandage for equality for women, but as inadequate in other areas, such as not assuring women of equal pay for equal work or automatically extending women's rights to men.

Schlafly, a Harvard Phi Beta Kappa graduate, was middle-class, Catholic, and the mother of six children. Her credentials lent her views authority and many family-oriented women listened. They saw themselves as the antithesis of the career-oriented, single feminists and accused the other side of wanting to destroy the family. Confusion set in between the sexes, and men were never quite sure whether a woman would allow him to open a door for her or whether it would be seen as an act of chauvinism, as most men did not want to be labeled with the term Chauvinist Pig.

DIFFICULT FUNDRAISING UNDER PRESSURE

Condemnation of male behavior heightened through the years, along with Friedan's criticisms of Gloria. In a speech at Trinity College in Hartford, Connecticut, Friedan told the audience that the media celebrated Gloria because of her looks, but that no one should mistake her for a leader of the movement. Later, Friedan accused Gloria of "ripping off the movement for profit."[17] Gloria had avoided controversy somewhat after the article in *Esquire* the previous year, but Friedan's words led Gloria to tell the press that furthering the women's movement had actually cost her money, although she felt that whatever she spent was well worth it. Friedan replied that her comments had been taken out of context and misquoted but did not make another statement to refute what she had said.

During the first part of the year, Gloria had worked with the *Ms.* staff to get a stand-alone issue onto newsstands by midyear, and with Harris out of the system, they were eager to pursue financing to allow the project to continue. Now, at least, they had leverage—a complete issue that had sold out in a short time with subscriptions waiting to be filled.

Clay Felker was out of the question as a backer, however. As a seasoned publishing veteran, he would insist that *New York* maintain control, but Gloria and Carbine would not hear of it. Earlier, they had contacted Warner Communications, but control continued to be an issue. Their first meeting produced no results, and Gloria and Carbine refused the initial offer, although they had asked for and were offered $3 million, with Warner in control. The ironic reality was that when they got back down to the street, they realized that they were asking for millions of dollars when neither of them had enough money to afford a cab. They had a good laugh over their audacity and when they arrived at Ms., they rushed inside and asked to borrow $5 for the cab waiting on the street below. Eventually, Warner did capitulate and agreed to invest $1 million for 25 percent of *Ms.* in the form of preferred stock, without the stipulation that Warner would maintain control. Warner continued to help with smaller loans in order to protect the company's investment.

When Ms. hit the streets in July, it had 56,000 subscribers. These subscribers had significant financial resources, were highly educated, and were considered to be well worth the investment of advertisers, trying to reach an upscale audience. Yet, the only funding from advertising the magazine got was from companies that made women's products, such as perfume, clothing, and makeup. Car companies, electronics firms, and credit grantors still shied away from women's magazines, deciding to put their dollars into advertising where the majority market was men. The mindset was that women did not buy cars, electronic equipment, or seek credit in their own names; the excuse that women did not understand technology was also part of this mindset.

Another big obstacle for Ms. was that Gloria and Carbine, along with the staff of Ms., wanted the magazine to remain issue oriented, not consumer product driven. For instance, food companies such as Nabisco, General Mills, Pillsbury, and Carnation wanted accompanying recipes in the magazine to promote their products. Ms. neither did recipes, nor cleaning tips or any homemaking advice or discussion. When Ms. acquired an account, the problem was further enhanced because Ms. refused to publish any ad that was demeaning to women. Gloria wrote, "We know we don't need those endless little editorial diagrams of where to put our lipstick or blush—we don't identify with all those airbrushed photos of skeletal women with everything about them credited, even their perfume.... "[18] So, the task of raising funds for the magazine was daunting and exhausting.

CONFUSING POLITICS

The entire spring that year was extremely grueling for Gloria; aside from Ms., she was also heavily involved in promoting the NWPC before the upcoming Democratic Convention to be held that summer. Her schedule was overfilled with writing, speaking, organizing, and trying to start a new magazine. The NWPC had held a Women's Education for Delegate Selection meeting earlier in the year to strategize getting more women delegates to each presidential convention, hoping to create women's caucuses and making it possible for women to convince candidates to voice their concerns in exchange for their votes. Gloria intended to be at the convention and to support two candidates.

Having been a longtime McGovern follower, Gloria endorsed his candidacy in February, but also wanting a woman to succeed, she endorsed Shirley Chisholm in March. She was criticized heavily for working for both candidates, and it caused a great deal of confusion. Whereas Gloria campaigned for McGovern only in states where Chisholm was not running, she chose Chisholm as her candidate in states where both competed for votes. In New York, for example, McGovern had to convince voters that Gloria was *not* on his side. Chisholm was unhappy that Gloria was not providing complete loyalty to her campaign. Gloria ran as a Chisholm delegate, as did Friedan; although Friedan lost, Gloria won, thereby intensifying Friedan's frustration.

However, a few weeks before the convention began, the two women did meet with McGovern to discuss women's issues. Also present was actress Shirley MacLaine, McGovern's campaign advisor on women's issues. Mc-Govern agreed to consider a plank in his platform regarding abortion, which had not yet been legalized, and it was to read: "The Democratic Party opposes government interference in the reproductive and sexual freedom of the individual American citizen."[19] Yet, Shirley MacLaine stepped in. She explained that the language of the plank put McGovern in a precarious position—it would defy states' rights regarding sex laws. She worried that a journalist would research the laws and would conclude that McGovern was for indiscriminate sex at large. Gloria disagreed, saying no one would notice and stuck to the language. When MacLaine found a series of proposals designed to go to the platform committee's task force with the stated abortion plank at the bottom, she got a pair of scissors and cut it off every sheet.

At the Democratic presidential convention in Miami, Gloria wrote Chisholm's major TV speech and continued to work for both candidates. Although she did what she thought best, she ended up displeasing both candidates and the women's caucus came away feeling as if they had been heard in part, but that their true concerns were ignored. To make matters worse, a week after the convention, Friedan ended up making her animosity toward Gloria blatantly public and their contention became part of early feminist lore.

Friedan accused Gloria and her like-minded followers, including the lesbians, of being man haters, which judging just by the number of close relationships Gloria had with men, was preposterous. Friedan biographer Daniel Horowitz wrote:

> At a July 1972 press conference announcing an article in a forthcoming issue of McCall's, [Friedan] denounced her detractors in the women's movement, including Abzug and Steinem, as "female chauvinist boors." She accused Steinem of fostering a "female chauvinism that makes a woman apologize for loving her husband and children." The result, Friedan claimed, was that her opponents were "corrupting our movement for equality and inviting a backlash that endangers the very real gains we have won these past few years." With these words and in her August article, Friedan, responding to the victory of Steinem and Abzug at the Democratic convention,

violated the understanding among feminists that they not attack one another in public.[20]

The snide remarks from Friedan did little to further the women's movement, but only undermined it. The common fallacy is that women cannot get along together, and here she was proving it through the media. She was also promoting family values over individuality, which split the movement in twain.

Yet, all politicking aside, Richard M. Nixon, the Republican Candidate for president, won the election in November. It seemed that all Gloria's hard work was being diluted, including *Ms.* magazine. She said, "[Newsman] Harry Reasoner went on television with a national review of the magazine, saying it could not possibly last for more than six months."[21] And the *New York Times* had called the women's movement "a passing fad."[22] Even after several years, "women's lib" still was not taken seriously.

NOTES

1. "Press Statement by the Women's Action Alliance," *Women's History Manuscripts* (Smith College), http://www.smith.edu/libraries/libs/ssc/curriculum/images/waa1-1z.jpg.

2. Quoted in Mary Thom, *Inside "Ms." 25 Years of the Magazine and the Feminist Movement* (New York: Henry Holt, 1997), p. 8.

3. Quoted in Judith Hennessee, *Betty Friedan, Her Life* (New York: Random House, 1999), p. 152.

4. Quoted in Thom, *Inside "Ms.,"* p. 12.

5. Ibid.

6. Ibid.

7. Hennessee, *Betty Friedan, Her Life*, p. 157.

8. Gloria Steinem, "The Politics of Women," commencement address to Smith College class of 1971, http://smith.alumnae.net/homepages/Classes/1971/gloria.html.

9. Steinem, interview, 27 January 2003.

10. Steinem, interview, 27 January 2003.

11. Katherine Graham, *Personal History* (New York: Vintage Books, 1997), p. 422.

12. Quoted in Hennessee, *Betty Friedan, Her Life*, p. 163.

13. Ibid., p. 168.

14. Quoted in Thom, *Inside "Ms.,"* p. 6.

15. Quoted in Hennessee, *Betty Friedan, Her Life*, p. 157.

16. Quoted in Heilbrun, *Education of a Woman*, p. 189.

17. Ibid.

18. Steinem, *Moving Beyond Words*, p. 126.

19. Quoted in Stern, *Gloria Steinem*, p. 244.

20. Daniel Horowitz, *Betty Friedan and the Making of the Feminine Mystique* (Amherst: University of Massachusetts Press, 1998), p. 235.

21. "Ms. 25th," interview with Gloria Steinem by Scott Simon, *Weekend Saturday*, National Public Radio, 20 September 1997.

22. Quoted in Heilbrun, *Education of a Woman*, p. 232.

Chapter 11

CATACLYSM AND CONTROVERSY

December of 1972 saw Gloria and her partners at Ms. preparing for a future, regardless of what others said. They knew the Ms. audience was loyal and they wanted a way to give back to the women who supported the magazine. As no foundations existed to give money expressly for women's causes, the Ms. Foundation was established that year, and meant to acquire any profits the magazine would accrue, along with various donations from other individuals and corporate entities.

Actor Marlo Thomas of *That Girl* (the first television show devoted to a single woman living alone in New York) conceived the project, which actually kicked off the Ms. Foundation's grants program—"Free to Be...You and Me," an NBC TV special that strove to challenge stereotypes and to promote the uniqueness of the individual. Many well-known personalities contributed to the project, including poet and writer Shel Silverstein, children's book illustrator Diane Dillon, writer Kurt Vonnegut, Jr., actor Alan Alda, and composer and actor Kris Kristopherson. The television show won an Emmy award, which led to print, electronic, and audio versions that continue to sell. Proceeds from the sale of the first album of "Free to Be...You and Me" were donated to the Ms. Foundation.

The following year saw major advances in causes for women. On January 22, 1973, the *Roe v. Wade* decision regarding legal abortion was handed down, allowing women to obtain legal abortions in the first three months of pregnancy. In February, the first woman to make the keynote speech at the Republican National Convention, Anne Armstrong, was also the first woman to be appointed to a president's cabinet. As counselor to President Nixon, one of her duties would be to appoint women to federal posts. The NWPC held its first national convention in February as well. And on September 20, world champion tennis player Billie Jean King defeated world champion tennis player Bobby Riggs in a highly publicized tennis match, called The Battle of the Sexes, for which Riggs held that a woman could never defeat a man in tennis or any other sport.

Yet, the year would be fraught with discovery of corruption in the government as the Watergate trials began. In March the so-called Watergate burglars, including G. Gordon Liddy and James W. McCord, Jr., were sentenced to jail terms for breaking into the Democratic headquarters and the office of defense analyst Daniel Ellsberg's psychiatrist. Ellsberg, who had copied a top secret document, known as the Pentagon Papers—a secret government study of decision making in the Vietnam War, involving five U.S. presidents—leaked the information to the Senate and the press in an attempt to stop the Vietnam War by alerting the public to the fact that presidents usually got their way, regardless of the decision's merit. The Watergate plumbers were trying to find information to use against Ellsberg, who had set the country on fire with these disclosures.

In connection with the Watergate burglary, top White House aides resigned in April 1974, including top advisors John Erlichman and H.R. Haldeman, along with the United States Attorney General Richard G. Kleindienst. Televised hearings were held, beginning in May, and the nation looked on, thoroughly disillusioned with the United States government.

Though the nation continued to suffer the effects of Watergate, the following year would bring several other important firsts for women. Helen Thomas was named the first woman White House correspondent for United Press International, and Julia Phillips won the first producer's academy award for her work on the movie The Sting, starring Robert Redford and Paul Newman. Already 1,000 colleges were offering women's studies programs, and the Episcopal Church ordained its first women priests.

Major changes continued throughout 1974, but the ultimate outrage of the Watergate fiasco culminated in the resignation of President Nixon, who allegedly participated in the ensuing cover-up. Vice President Gerald Ford—who had assumed office in November 1973 after Vice President Spiro Agnew resigned in order to avoid charges of income tax evasion—took his oath of office on the ninth of August. He became the first president to meet with representatives of NOW and members of 16 other women's groups from around the nation. Things were surely looking up for feminism, and for the first time, Ms. magazine actually earned a profit.

ATTACK FROM BEHIND

Not much changed for Gloria for the next two years. She continued to speak on behalf of the women's movement, to meet with company executives in order to fund Ms. magazine, and generally ran herself ragged. One of Gloria's finest qualities is kindness, a willingness to help others in need—especially other women—even at the expense of her own comfort. She was also known for giving much of her income to one cause or another and still lived out of stacked boxes in her apartment. She could not settle her living space because she was not settled, not personally or professionally. It seemed that everything Gloria did was last minute and demanding of her, emotionally and physically.

At the pinnacle of this incredible stress for Gloria came a devastating blow, and it came from inside the women's movement. When the *Ramparts* magazine article appeared regarding the NSA's involvement with the CIA in 1967, Gloria had been asked to field questions from reporters, as she had been the public relations person for the conference in Vienna. It led to an appearance on the *CBS Evening News* with Walter Cronkite, where Gloria explained how the conference had been set up by the Soviets for purposes of propaganda. She also described how the NSA, by then the IRS, had funded American students' participation and cultural exhibits, hoping to shed positive light on democracy.

Gloria had also discussed the CIA link openly with the *New York Times*, saying that CIA funding was necessary due to the atmosphere of McCarthyism in the 1950s. Funding from other sources was impossible to obtain, as corporations and foundations wanted to maintain their distance from anything having to do with communism.

These candid remarks led to an article in the *Washington Post*, declaring that Gloria had worked extensively with the CIA, but also admitting that the CIA had never tried to change IRS policy, to report on the people involved in the festival, or to report on foreign participants. But in another interview with the *Washington Post*, Gloria told reporters, "In my experience the Agency [the CIA] was completely different from its image; it was liberal, nonviolent, and honorable."[1] To Gloria, the NSA had simply acquired the needed funds to actively participate in a worthwhile endeavor.

Yet, the CIA had become even more repulsive to many Americans, which was under scrutiny for plotting the assassinations of various political leaders around the world by 1975. From Vietnam, news of CIA agents killing and torturing any suspected agents of the National Liberation

Front (NLF or Viet Cong) shocked mainstream America; ergo, any affiliations with the CIA fell under the agency's dark shadow.

On May 9, 1975, the Redstockings reunified and called a press conference at a convention held by *More*, a liberal journalists' magazine. During the proceedings, they issued a 16-page document entitled, "Redstockings Discloses Gloria Steinem's CIA Cover-Up." The treatise confirmed that they had obtained information to show that Gloria had had a 10-year association with the CIA between 1959 and 1969, and it accused her of hiding her association. They also maintained that she was a CIA secret weapon, intent on destroying the women's movement, and that her vehicle for doing that was *Ms.* magazine. However, they left room to suggest that Gloria might also be promoting corporate or rich and powerful interests in her mission to derail women's liberation.

Evidence for their claims came from various sources. They asserted that Gloria's association with *Ms.* magazine, the Women's Action Alliance, and the National Black Feminist Organization, provided her with a list of names and information about women involved in the movement to use surreptitiously. It also stated that Pat Carbine's remarks on a television show that the women's movement was currently in phase two, meant not Second Wave, but rather that the radicals had had their day and that the rationals had taken over. They accused Clay Felker, who had worked with Gloria in Helsinki, of rejecting an article that was critical of *Ms.*, and they were miffed that *Ms.* had diluted the image of Wonder Woman, which appeared on the second cover of the magazine, by making her a conservative pacifist: rather than wielding her "golden lasso," Wonder Woman was shown racing through city traffic, holding a shopping bag, past storefronts reading "Peace ~ Justice '72." The report read, "Gloria Steinem has a history of gathering information for the Central Intelligence Agency. She has been dishonest in the past about this and is still covering it up. She has therefore not earned the trust her present position requires."[2]

TRANSITION IN THE MIDST OF ADVERSITY

The Redstockings' treatise was to be included in a book the group was about to publish. Journalists eagerly gathered up the information provided, hoping to break a big story. However, once they studied the materials, most of them decided the Redstockings had fabricated the conspiracy from yesterday's news and dropped the subject. However, a few feminist publications did clamor for Gloria's response.

Gloria was devastated and felt that the animosity was prompted by a failed attempt by Kathie Sarachild, leader of the reformed Redstockings, to edit an anthology of consciousness-raising articles for Ms. Sarachild argued with Ms. editors over control and content, and the finished manuscript was considered to be unpublishable. Gloria told Sarachild this and said that she could keep the advance, unless she found another publisher. Since the manuscript was never published, Gloria sees the rejection as proof that the manuscript was not marketable material. Gloria considers Sarachild's attack to have been a personal vendetta.

To no one's great surprise, Friedan jumped into the fray to support the Redstockings and began speaking out against Gloria's supposed connection to the CIA in public. When the first story about the incident came out in the *New York Daily News*, a quote from Betty was included: "I was very troubled by the Redstockings' statements, and so were a lot of other people I know. . . . I don't see how she [Gloria] can ignore these charges. She can't ignore them."[3] She was also eager to discuss the allegations with the International Women's Year conference in Mexico City on June 19, but was persuaded against doing so.

Gloria maintained silence. She was stunned at what had been termed the trashing. The attacks she had received from the press had been hurtful, media-driven events. Friedan's attacks were more like sibling rivalry, and Gloria tolerated them in good humor. Yet, the CIA accusations had come from the Redstockings, an organization that was part of her world, and one that she had respected. It seemed like a blind-side blow. Feminism was her life. She had given major portions of herself to the movement. The work she had done in spreading the message had expended her physical energy, and the attack was just too much. Gloria was devastated.

She had also recently ended her long-term relationship with Franklin Thomas, when they both decided they were too much alike. However, they remained friendly, as she did with all her ex-beaus. Gloria had a knack for keeping breakups amicable; either she casually slid away from her partner, or the relationships ended by mutual choice.

Stan Pottinger, the U.S. attorney general for civil rights at the time (now a novelist), had come into Gloria's life, and the couple had what Gloria called a little marriage, as she viewed most of her long-term relationships. Although both parties kept their own living spaces, Pottinger and Gloria lived together on weekends, in Washington (where he was based) or in New York (Gloria's home), with Stan's two oldest children, who lived with him. Gloria enjoyed his children, as they did Gloria for her ability to talk to them without condescension.

Pottinger helped Gloria through the bad stretch she had encountered, as did many of her friends. Regarding her response to the Redstockings's and then Friedan's attacks, she asked several of them what they thought she should do. Most of them advised her to keep silent about the situation. By answering the charges, most thought she would only attract more media hype. Joanne Edgar, Gloria's assistant, fielded most of the inquiries, and Gloria stayed quiet.

A LONG-AWAITED ANSWER

Finally, in September, Gloria wrote a six-page letter and sent it to six feminist newspapers, along with supporting letters from Redstockings founding members, who were not part of the new group, including Rita Mae Brown and Robin Morgan. Her action was prompted by another article, which appeared in the *New York Times*, written by Lucinda Franks. Gloria refused to be interviewed regarding the CIA issue, and Franks' article rehashed the situation all over again. Gloria was pressured to respond for the sake of the movement.

However, the situation had vexed Gloria throughout the summer months and she had become very thin and distraught. Because of her physical and emotional condition, she botched her letter to the press and continued to strengthen her detractors' suspicions. "I naïvely thought then that the ultimate money source didn't matter, since in my own experience, no control or orders came with it," wrote Steinem.[4] Yet, what she wrote could not dispel the grey haze hanging over her.

Eventually, Gloria regained her composure and went about changing the world again. The year 1976 meant another presidential election and Democratic convention. Gloria wrote in her "City Politic" column for *New York* that she intended to leave town when the convention started, as it was to be held in New York City. She felt that she had done her part as an activist and wrote that she had testified at Platform Committee hearings, attended NWPC meetings, and helped with the '76 Democratic Women's Agenda. She indicated that she had thought that it was time for other feminists to take up the challenge.

Yet, when the convention actually happened, Gloria was amidst the fray. By 1976, women had found acceptance in the party and evolved into a genuine lobby. The media gave greater respect to the women's contingent, and the delegates were able to demonstrate solidarity. Gloria remarked, "Whatever the disagreements internally, we bargained as a unit, and were treated seriously by the candidate as the same."[5] When Jimmy

Carter won the nomination for president, and subsequently the desk in the Oval Office, he appointed many women to significant positions.

In early 1977, Gloria was in high demand for public speaking. Although the appearances helped her to make a difference, which was her lifetime goal, the road wearied her. Yet, she continued to press on.

On March 28, Bella Abzug was appointed to preside over the National Commission on the Observation of International Women's Year. Also named to the commission were former First Lady Betty Ford, civil rights activist Coretta Scott King, poet Maya Angelou, and many other prominent women, including Gloria. A National Women's Conference would take place in Houston in July. From that point on, Gloria's focus would be the convention.

When the conference opened in Houston on July 18, it began with the passing of a lighted torch, which had been relayed from Seneca Falls, New York, home of the Women's Hall of Fame and where the first Women's Rights Convention had been held in 1848. Fifteen thousand women attended the conference, and among them were two thousand national convention delegates.

AN OPPORTUNITY TO WRITE

Although Gloria knew the work she did was important, she had always had the personal desire to simply write. Her ambition to write a book about the impact of feminism on political theory was a driving force when she applied for a Woodrow Wilson Fellowship, which offered a safe haven for writing without interruption at the Woodrow Wilson Center in Washington, D.C. The fellowship also included a stipend of $30,255 to subsidize the writer's living expenses while at the center. A year away from the hectic pace of activism seemed the perfect solution to Gloria's exhaustion and the fulfillment of a dream—she had wanted to write a book for a very long time.

Yet, Gloria's ambitions for her project connected to the Woodrow Wilson fellowship were overstated, even for someone so capable of doing the work. *Feminism and Its Impact of the Premises and Goals of Current Political Theory* would make an extraordinary book; however, it would require extraordinary discipline to complete in only one year, even if she did nothing but write four to six hours a day and was uninterrupted by daily life. The situation was impossible, as she still had material responsibilities at *Ms.* and planned to spend Thursdays and Fridays in New York. The Woodrow Wilson Center also expected Gloria to participate in daily seminars and luncheons, which the fellowship's benefactors required to promote a scholarly atmosphere. As Gloria was one of few women to attend, they felt that her presence was highly important.

Never the one for conventionality, Gloria asked that a cot be placed in her office. Writers often have a special time of day when they are most creative and productive, and Gloria's was at night. She often found it necessary to nap on the cot during the day, while the other fellows were hard at work.

She was not able to spend regular hours at the center, either, as Ms. magazine was in trouble. Still finding it difficult to obtain sufficient advertising income, the magazine was deeply in debt and losing money. Gloria and Carbine were not ready to relinquish editorial control of the magazine, which prevented them from securing investors, who would undoubtedly want a percentage of the administrational power. After much discussion with several advisors, Gloria and Carbine had a solution—Ms. would become a nonprofit foundation, a subsidiary of the Ms. Foundation. In this way, the magazine could accept donations and save money on postage due to the nonprofit status of the organization.[6] In addition, the Ford Foundation was set to make a major contribution, if the magazine went in this direction.

All of this change at Ms. kept Gloria busy in addition to living up to her commitment to the Woodrow Wilson fellowship, and that end of the bargain was suffering. The director of the center was so aghast at her behavior and her sporadic attention that he wrote to Gloria in March 1978: "I would be inclined to encourage a slight increase in participation and collegial activities here."[7]

Of course Gloria responded respectfully, but also laid out her opposition to the director's suggestion. She wrote back that the luncheons were a chore and that she was tired of answering questions on women's point of view, as she was not there to conduct a class on feminism. She was burdened further by uninterested but lascivious men, who would bring up any topic just to speak to an attractive woman. She was also passionately involved in the fight for the ERA, on which NOW had recently declared a state of emergency, and continued to speak out on reproductive freedom, as she labeled her pro-choice stance. She wrote that she had come into the program simply to write, without interruption, and was sorry that the program was nothing like she had envisioned.

CLASHES WITH THE RELIGIOUS RIGHT AND AN END TO A DREAM

Gloria was also at odds with the religious conservatives at the time. The Moral Majority, led by Jerry Falwell, and the Catholic Church were the movement's harshest enemies. Staunchly anti-ERA, pro-life, and against women's lib, the groups were also anti-Gloria, the missionary of the movement. But not all members of the Catholic Church had equal sentiments. Catholic nuns wanted women to have the right to be priests, and some Catholic priests were for birth control and even abortion, two actions severely condemned by the church.

Father Harvey Egan of St. Joan of Arc Church in Minneapolis asked Gloria to present a homily to his congregation. She was not the first guest speaker he had invited who had a liberal point of view, nor was she the first woman. Yet, some of the locals and the hierarchy of the Catholic Church were outraged when Egan allowed the opposition to have a voice in Gloria. Mobs gathered before the church screaming, "She is a murderer!" and "Gloria Steinem is a baby killer."[8]

Yet, in her two homily sessions, Gloria did not use the term *abortion*. She merely stated that it should be the individual's right to choose, without government interference, whether or not to have children. She said that the decision to reproduce was an inalienable right, just as important as the rights to free speech or assembly. She also pointed out that a patriarchal institution was controlling women in the church.

Headlines blazoned across the country, making it necessary for Gloria to state her position on *CBS Morning News,* as did Egan. Egan's archbishop John Roach referred to Gloria's speech as an affront to pro-lifers. However, there was support for Gloria and Egan from an unexpected arena, when Gloria was invited by an Episcopal minister to speak at his church. Egan's parishioners also showed support for him by increased attendance at services. However, Pope Paul VI gave his opinion of the situation in a dictum forbidding laypersons to give homilies in any Catholic church.

By October, the director of the Woodrow Wilson Center was again writing to Gloria to complain that someone had used her ID and key to work after hours in her office. He also stated that he had read of her outside activities of late and hoped that she was taking no more than three days a week away from the center. Gloria responded by writing that she had appreciated the opportunity to work at the center over the year, but that she was near acceptance of a separate book contract, was pursuing publication, and would not finish her fellowship project. She offered to return part of the stipend.

POLITICS AND EX-PORN STARS

Resuming her prefellowship life, the year 1979 was a political year for Gloria, as she busied herself organizing yet another political action committee. Voters for Choice (VFC) began with board members from *Ms.* magazine and Planned Parenthood, and meant to support candidates of any party that took a pro-choice stance. Gloria wrote, "A woman's right to choose is under attack and should not be taken for granted. Who we elect to office matters."[9] Today, VFC is the only national organization providing this type of support.

That year ERA matters came to a head, and Gloria was frustrated with explaining the meaning of the simple legislation—equal rights for all— and blamed the media for presenting the right-wing opinions of Phyllis Schlafly, as equal time rules required, without bothering to investigate the implications of her accusations. Gloria continued to assert that the ERA implied nothing about drafting women or changes in the social security laws. Yet, the deadline for ratification was March 22 and confirmation was in doubt.

Just as a bill was introduced in Congress, proposing to extend the ratification deadline, Katherine Graham asked Gloria to speak to the editorial board of the *Washington Post*. Graham hoped that Gloria could sway board members to sponsor the extension, as positive support in the *Post* might boost congressional backing for the measure. Although Gloria had become more comfortable as a speaker, certain audiences panicked her and the editorial board of the *Washington Post* was one of them. She remembers the experience as one of the worst in her life, due to her fear of speaking in public. The knowledge that her speech would be important to the success of the ERA made it a crucial discussion, and in addition to that, board members were the elite in her professional field and their opinions counted in Washington. Gloria was not able to sway them, but they still got the extension; however, it would ultimately expire on June 30, 1982, coming three states short of those needed for ratification. The fight for the ERA continues to the present day.

In 1980, Gloria published her first essay involving former porn star Linda Lovelace, who had appeared in the film *Deep Throat* in 1972. Linda Boreman Marchiano (Lovelace's real name) claimed to have been physically and psychologically abused by her husband manager, Chuck Traynor, for several years. When Gloria saw the woman on a television talk show, she had compassion for her plight and decided that she wanted to help Marchiano to regain her self-image.

During the time the film was popular, the general population, rather than only those interested in pornography, had accepted it. *Deep Throat* had cost only $40,000 thousand to make, but grossed over $600 million in tickets, rentals, and merchandise; yet, Marchiano received only $1,200 for her performance. Linda Lovelace had become a pop culture icon, but Linda Marchiano had become a sexual slave. She claimed to have been beaten, repeatedly raped, and treated as chattel—an extreme example of patriarchal domination, which was totally unacceptable to Gloria.

When Gloria read Marchiano's book *Ordeal,* in which she disclosed the horrible circumstances under which she had lived and how she escaped, Gloria immediately offered Marchiano her support, though Marchiano had no idea who Gloria was at the time. Gloria invited her to spend some time at the *Ms.* offices to learn more about feminism and to meet other feminists. Gloria also wrote about Marchiano's victimization in the May 1980 issue of *Ms.* and continued to support her, until Marchiano's death in a traffic accident in April 2002.

Many significant changes occurred in 1981, both personal and political, for Gloria. She was appalled by the old boy network atmosphere surrounding President Ronald Reagan's administration and felt that his actions toward women were destructive. In July, his administration announced plans to roll back federal antidiscrimination regulations. *Feminist.org* reported, "The effect of which would undo twenty years of progress for women. . . . [The assault ranged] from proposals to ease job bias regulations affecting thirty million American employees to weakening guidelines that protected women from sexual harassment, and undermining protections against sex discrimination in educational institutions."[10]

SADNESS ACCOMPANIED BY THE LAST LAUGH

As feminists were pleased with the 1981 nomination of former Senate Majority Leader Sandra Day O'Connor as the first woman associate justice to serve on the Supreme Court of the United States on July 7, Gloria was saddened by the death of her mother around that time. Ruth had lived in a nursing home for two years before her death from a stroke. Although her death was not a shock to Gloria, as Ruth was approaching her 82nd birthday and had not been well in some time, the loss of a mother is typically difficult for women. Gloria loved her mother very much and felt the loss deeply.

Because Ruth loved the Episcopalian church in Washington, her daughters held a service for her there. The church was well known for helping the poor, had a woman priest, and had welcomed Ruth with affection. Gloria and Susanne also made sure that her obituary reported that Ruth had been a writer, as that is how she would like to be remembered.

Yet, Gloria quickly filed the sad event in her personal mind—the mind that only select others were allowed to penetrate. She continued fighting for the ERA, working for Ms., working for the VFC and the NWPC, and continued trying to squeeze spare moments in for herself to write. Writing was still Gloria's first love.

July 1982 brought Ms. magazine's 10th anniversary, proving Harry Reasoner doubly wrong in his assessment that the magazine would not last five years. A double issue was planned, and it was decided that Gloria had to be on the cover. Yet, they did not want her to pose alone, but with a group of women, representing those of different ages, races, and occupations. They also tied in new subscription solicitations to her speaking engagements. As she arrived in a city, a batch of postcards arrived asking for new subscribers, and the plan worked very well. The subscription offers that ran in the issue were also quite successful, giving Ms. a terrific boost. And in the media, talk show host Phil Donohue devoted an entire show to discussing the magazine, while the Today Show did segments on it for a week. There was also a party with 1,200 guests. Ms. had become an icon of modern society.

The success of Ms. propelled Gloria into New York magazine's list of influential women that year. In league with Sandra Day O'Connor; Katherine Graham; tennis star Billy Jean King; and Eleanor Smeal, president of NOW at the time, who placed in the four top spots, Gloria tied with Phyllis Schlafly for fifth place.

Continuing her fame and popularity, Outrageous Acts and Other Rebellions, Gloria's second book, was published in 1983. Many works in the collection of essays previously appeared in other publications. She included her article "I Was a Playboy Bunny," from 20 years earlier, as well as articles on campaigning, her college reunion, Marilyn Monroe, former First Lady Patricia Nixon, and Linda Lovelace. Yet, her most poignant essay was new, about her mother. In "Ruth's Song (Because She Could Not Sing It)," Gloria finally exposed the tragedy of her childhood and exonerated her parents in writing for the loneliness of the years she spent as a child trying to cope with a delusional mother. She lays the blame on society and once said in a televised interview with ABC News, "It wasn't that she was mentally ill. I realized everything she loved had been taken away from her. She fell into an incredible depression. It was not her fault. It could have happened to anyone in similar circumstances."[11]

Ruth had wanted to be a writer and had professional success before marrying Leo; yet, the moment she became a wife, society dictated that she follow her husband and bear his children. Moving to Clark Lake, being isolated from her family and friends, and giving up her job at the

Toledo Blade were actions expected of Ruth, and her years of black depression over never being the person she wanted to be obviously affected Gloria tremendously.

But the book never would have happened if Letty Cottin Pogrebin had not coordinated the essays for Gloria and sold the book. However, *Outrageous Acts* is dedicated to many others including,

> Robert Benton, whose long-ago listening to stories of a Toledo childhood helped show me that I needn't pretend to be someone else to be a writer; to Clay Felker, who never cared what gender of journalist a newsworthy idea came from; to the Woodrow Wilson International Center for Scholars at the Smithsonian Institution, whose fellowship provided time for much of the research herein; to Stan Pottinger for eight years of friendship, encouragement, and vitality... to my father, Leo Steinem, who taught me to love and live with insecurity; to my mother, Ruth Nuneviller Steinem, who performed the miracle of loving others even when she could not love herself.... [12]

In a single dedication, Gloria had summed up much of her past.

NOTES

1. Quoted in Stern, *Gloria Steinem*, p. 292.

2. Ibid., p. 295.

3. Quoted in Hennessee, *Betty Friedan, Her Life*, p. 210.

4. Susan E. Reed, "Sisterhood Was Powerful," *The American Prospect* 11, (17 July 2000), pp. 41–43.

5. Quoted in Heilbrun, *Education of a Woman*, p. 312.

6. Regulations on free postage for nonprofit organizations would change in later years.

7. Quoted in Heilbrun, *Education of a Woman*, p. 331.

8. Ibid., p. 333.

9. Gloria Steinem, "A Message from Gloria," *Voters for Choice*, http://www.voters4choice.org/.

10. "The Feminist Chronicles."

11. Gloria Steinem, on *Upclose Tonight*, interview by Michelle Martin, ABC-NEWS.com, 15 January 2003, http://abcnews.go.com/sections/UpClose/DailyNews/Gloria_Steinem_Email.html.

12. Steinem, *Outrageous Acts*, p. vii.

Chapter 12

CHANGES FOR A BETTER LIFE

Early in 1983, Gloria sold the rights of her article "A Bunny's Tale" to producer Joan Marks, who had wanted to make a movie of Gloria's Playboy experiences for television. Though Gloria did not write the screenplay, part of her deal included script approval. She wanted to be sure the movie version of what happened did not deviate too far from the reality and that it did not turn into a voyeuristic farce for the aggrandizement of men wanting only to see the Bunny actors in skimpy costumes.[1]

Also in 1983, Gloria made several personal television appearances and received some backlash from the media. She hosted a Lifetime Television series, entitled *A Conversation with . . .* and appeared on an NBC comedy special—*The News Is the News,* for which she suffered the barbs of CBS's Andy Rooney. He ridiculed her professionally streaked hair and makeup, telling his audience that her appearance was not consistent with feminist ideals. Gloria simply responded by saying that everyone on the show was wearing the same makeup and mentioned that any detractors of the feminist movement would immediately attack a feminist's looks, regardless of their level of attractiveness. Then, she was included in Mr. Blackwell's "10 Worst Dressed List of 1984," to which she nonchalantly retorted, "I was disturbed until I realized there's only one thing that's worse—appearing on the 'Best Dressed' list."[2]

The second quarter of that year was a transitional period for Gloria. She celebrated her 50th birthday on March 25. She had taken up a new fitness routine that included exercise and a healthy diet, which she had been denied due to her constantly fast-paced lifestyle. Yet, she was still on a treadmill of too many things to do and not enough time in which to do them. Between writing, personal appearances for her book, the women's movement, and Ms. magazine, Gloria had very little personal life, and her interests were sapping her strength and energy.

Gloria simply gave to others day after day, nonstop. She donated not only her time, but also her money, as she enjoyed giving people who needed it a perk; however, with the publication of *Outrageous Acts*, her attorney advised her that she had better make plans for the future. They decided to set up a corporation—East Toledo Productions—as an initial act toward financial security. She also wanted a way to back projects in the community and establishing a corporation would give her a way to do that. Gloria finally realized that joking about giving her money away and becoming a bag lady in her 70s was not a joke anymore.

A BIRTHDAY BASH

Knowing Gloria's penchant for donating to one cause or another, Gloria's friends, including Marlo Thomas, Letty Pogrebin, and Suzanne Levine of Ms., decided they would help her to do it. Since they had traditionally strived to keep their parties at low cost, they decided to break from the norm and go black tie for Gloria's milestone birthday in the grand ballroom of the Waldorf-Astoria. However, they also used the occasion to raise money for Ms. Magazine and the Ms. Foundation at the expense of $250 a plate. Around 800 guests arrived, including hosts Marlo Thomas and Phil Donohue, civil rights activist Rosa Parks, Bella Abzug, Dolores Huerta, and singer Bette Midler, who donated her performance to the evening. Gloria remarked, "I thought, Why not? When I die, my funeral will be a benefit, too."[3]

Gloria went through another change very close to this time. Although Stan Pottinger had accompanied Gloria to her party, Mortimer (Mort) Zuckerman attended as a guest. She had been seeing both men for more than a month, but Zuckerman was not Gloria's usual date. He was a real estate magnet and magazine publisher at the time and not known for his integrity. (Today, he is editor in chief and publisher of *U.S. News and World Report* and owns Boston Properties, Inc.) Most of Gloria's friends were astounded when she began the relationship with him, although she told them he was the smartest man she ever knew and that she was obsessed with him.

But Gloria admits she was deluding herself. Zuckerman was not really the attraction; the incredible luxury of his enormous wealth soothed her exhaustion. She wrote, "Though I was privileged to be working in this movement that had given me life and friends I loved, I had less and less time to replenish lost energy—or even pick up my dry cleaning. Pressure is cumulative."[4] Zuckerman took care of everything for her; she did not have to think for a while. "He made every social decision (via his staff), so all I had to do was show up.... Since I had been helplessly recreating my caretaking pattern left over from childhood, he seemed the perfect answer: someone I *couldn't* take care of."[5]

After Gloria regained some of her strength, she realized the relationship was not a good one. She found that she had changed herself to suit Zuckerman's expectations of her and it was creating a rift with her chosen family of co-workers and old lovers. "I made all the classic errors of romance, including one I'd never made before: loving someone for what I *needed* instead of for what *he was.*"[6] Gloria graciously admits that the dissolution of the relationship was her doing. "I had deceived him by deceiving myself, and I'm still working on what I learned. But I do know that I chose an opposite as a dramatic example of what I missed in myself. Even allowing for me dissembling, perhaps that's what he was doing, too."[7]

One positive aspect of the relationship with Zuckerman is that she had more time to write. At Zuckerman's beach house, during the summer of 1985, she wrote most of her book *Marilyn, Norma Jeane*, a biography of Marilyn Monroe. She had written about Monroe for *Ms.* in August of 1972, and her publisher of *Outrageous Acts* at Henry Holt had asked for her expertise. He wanted her to work with George Barris, a photographer who had conducted a brief interview and had taken shots of Marilyn just before she died in 1962. Gloria thought the project would be interesting. She empathized with Marilyn, as she tended to do with all tragic women's souls. However, she had the impression that the publisher wanted only captions to the pictures and when the contract arrived, she realized that he expected 60,000 words, which would translate into about 200 printed pages.

Gloria took on the project, hoping to shed some light in a feminist direction, and wrote: "The goal of this project, therefore, could and should be closer to that of feminism in general: to include the viewpoints and influence of both women and men, and this to have a better chance of seeing one woman's life as a whole."[8] She found a personal connection to Monroe in that both shared neglected childhoods and both were forced outside their homes to find what they needed in life.

AN UNEXPECTED BATTLE

Also during her relationship with Zuckerman, a great deal of rumor circulated that Gloria was rushing to fertility specialists, trying to get pregnant. As she had been dead set against marrying and had always been adamantly opposed to having children herself, courting pregnancy seemed like hypocrisy to those who believed the rumors. The truth was, she had no intention of having a child. She had cancer.

The problem began in November of 1985, when Gloria found a lump in her breast. When her doctor evaluated the lump, she diagnosed it to be a fibroid adenoma, a benign tumor. Yet, a mammogram showed nothing. When she had a sonogram for the lump in her breast, once again, there were no untoward results. Gloria had always taken her health for granted, slept little, ate all the wrong things, and had no history of cancer. By May of 1996, her stress level was reaching the breaking point, and the whole situation depressed her.

Suzanne Levine, an editor at Ms., and her husband were good friends of Gloria's. They saw the incredible load she bore and suggested that she speak to a therapist. At her level of self-regard and exhaustion, she decided they might be right and tried to enter her sessions with an open mind. She saw Nancy Napier, author of Recreating Your Self, who helped her get in touch with her inner child.

Around the same time, Gloria's pretaped interviews of Cher, Robert Redford, Marlo Thomas, and others, along with features on social issues, began to appear on the Today Show on NBC television. Her segments were so well received that the producer asked if Gloria would like to sit in as coanchor for a week, while Jane Pauley, the regular host, was off on maternity leave. Although the idea of live television frightened her, Gloria agreed. To help her appearance by allowing her to wear contact lenses instead of glasses, she had eyelid surgery to remove excess fat from drooping lids in a simple office procedure.

In May 1986, on the Friday before the week she was to begin coanchoring on Today, Gloria had another regular checkup at the doctor's office and this time, learned that she had breast cancer. For Gloria, as for any woman learning they have cancer for the first time, the news was devastating. Still, she had agreed to do a job and went on with her television assignment. She kept the state of her health quiet, as she was worried that advertisers might pull away from Ms. if they felt she was ill and would have no part in the shape of the magazine. At the end of her week on Today, the producer told her she had done okay, which she took to mean not well. "I felt like saying, 'Well, not too badly considering I just got a diagnosis of breast cancer.' "[9]

In connection with her ailment, Gloria saw another physician for a second opinion, and it was determined that further surgery would be necessary to assure that any malignancy had been removed and to check the lymph nodes under her arm to be sure the disease had not spread. She chose to have a lumpectomy at Boston's Beth Israel Hospital, performed by Dr. William Silen, known for his advanced views on the treatment of breast cancer. Her friend Susan Levine accompanied her. Gloria was hospitalized, using the name Marie Ochs to keep her malady a secret. She stayed only two days, and the healing process was normal; however, she still had to travel to Sloan-Kettering hospital in New York every day for six weeks to have radiation therapy. At the time, she appreciated the convenience of Zuckerman's limousine. She would not reveal her ordeal to the public for two more years.

Gloria reevaluated her life after the breast cancer scare and came to three valuable self-realizations: first, that she had not been able to be a child and was obliged to mother her mother; second, that dodging the Toledo syndrome was not as easy as she had anticipated, realizing that Ms. magazine and its constant needs had assumed the role of her mother; and third, that she continued to repeat childhood patterns—not owning, not saving, and not caring for herself.

RESTRUCTURING LIFE

Her apartment was a perfect metaphor for her life. She put little value on taking time to decorate or even unpack, and she had not made time to do it. Her first mission after she recovered was to make changes in her living space. In March 1987, she also signed contracts to produce two books. She was advanced $700,000 from Little, Brown for a book on self-esteem and $500,000 from Simon and Schuster for a book on rich women. She used the money to make herself a home. She bought the apartment below hers with part of the money and made two large rooms into a study-den and a den-bedroom. She connected the ground floor by adding a narrow circular staircase.

Also that year, Gloria and Carbine had reluctantly decided that the only way they could keep Ms. on the newsstands and the message of feminism alive was to sell the magazine. In June, Fairfax Publications (U.S.) Ltd. became its new owners. The original owners were pleased to relay magazine operations to two women—Sandra Yates, president of Fairfax, and Anne Summers, Ms.'s new editor. The transaction was finalized in November 1987 for $10 million, part in cash and part through the payment of Ms.'s liabilities. Yet, the sale did not stick. The Fairfax company ran into trouble and had to sell Ms. again to pay off its debts. But Yates and Summers were so committed to Ms. and to Sassy, a young adult magazine also owned by Fairfax, that they decided to form their own corporation, Matilda Publications, and buy out Fairfax. However, Sassy tackled hard issues for teens, such as AIDS, losing one's virginity, and abortion, and many traditionally minded advertisers pulled away from the magazine, once again causing a cash deficit for the company. By June 1989, Matilda sold Ms. once again to Dale Lang, the owner of Working Woman and Working Mother.

Yet, Lang had the idea to stop publication of Ms. and to shift its audience to Working Woman or Working Mother. Gloria, who was still receiving a consulting salary at Ms., stepped in to attack his plan. Upon her objection, Lang offered to publish an eight-page newsletter, six times a year, but Gloria saw it only as a way to placate subscribers who did not want to switch to one of the working publications. She was upset that the proposed newsletter would lack letters, fiction, and poetry. She asked instead that Lang support an advertising-free Ms., with the costs to be covered by subscribers and newsstand sales, and Lang agreed to look into the proposal's feasibility.

Ruth Bower, the publisher of Ms. at the time, concluded that the magazine would have to be a bimonthly publication and that subscriptions would cost $40 a year, a steep price for a magazine subscription. But the women trusted their readers to keep Ms. a going concern and sent out survey cards, asking if they'd pay to keep Ms. running, with feminist writer Robin Morgan as its editor. A check in the yes box was a choice for a one-year subscription. The group anticipated only a two to three percent response, as is typical of this type survey. Yet, a whopping 19.8 percent of readers responded and Lang was convinced. For the first time, in 1991, Ms. ran in the black.

In 1992, Revolution from Within, a Book of Self Esteem, Gloria's work on realizing that integrating the interior self and the exterior self is vital in achieving self-worth was published, and the reviews were not stellar. The book was treated as Gloria's therapy journal by the press, but readers bought it for the autobiographical nature of the book, wanting not help for themselves, but to know more about Gloria. Others bought it in hopes of finding their way to feminism. The book leapt onto the bestseller lists and sold about 200,000 copies in the first month.[10]

To further enhance sales of Revolution from Within, Gloria's publisher set her up on a 26 city, 9-week publicity tour. All went well, until she wrote an article for People magazine, which included a 2-page shot of 49-year-old Gloria in a bubble bath with one leg extended, a typically sexy pose. As one who claimed never to have traded on her good looks, Gloria's permission to photograph her in such a suggestive situation was shocking. She claimed to have done it to show American readers that feminism did not mean unattractive.

AMENDING A CONTRACT

Still on tour for *Revolution from Within*, Gloria decided that she did not want to write the book on rich women. Yet, upon suggestion of returning her advance, Simon and Schuster told her that they still wanted a book, especially after the tremendous success of *Revolution from Within* in the marketplace. So, publisher and writer came to an agreement. Gloria would write a collection of essays, including one on rich women, to satisfy the previous agreement.

In January 1993, Amy Richards, who had been Gloria's assistant while attending Barnard, moved into Gloria's apartment to be a house sitter and to feed Gloria's cat, Magritte, but she ended up becoming a full-time housemate. Amy had helped Gloria in administering to the writing of *Revolution from Within*, along with Diana James, another of Gloria's personal assistants, who all worked at Gloria's to get her book done. She had run way over the deadline, as is Gloria's usual fault due to her unbelievably hectic schedule. Along with the other two women, another friend, Beth Rashbaum, appeared sometimes late in the evening to work with the team, and a fact checker, Mary Beth Guyther, also worked several nights a week. Gloria's new work, *Moving Beyond Words*, would be a similar scenario. Although Gloria had not stopped traveling and speaking, she had less to do with Ms., which afforded her only the slightest amount of time. Her schedule always fills quickly.

Three articles in *Moving Beyond Words* were new; the others were recycles from published works such as "Sex, Lies, and Advertising," which originally appeared in Ms. in 1990. But the final essay was "Doing Sixty," a work about Gloria approaching the sexagenarian stage of life. She summed up much in this quote:

> I used to indulge in magical thinking when problems seemed insurmountable. Often, this focused on men, for they seemed to be the only ones with power to intercede with the gods. Now it has been so long since I fantasized a magical rescue that I can barely remember the intensity of that longing. Instead, I feel my own strength, take pleasure in the company of

mortals, and no longer believe in gods. Except those in each of us.[11]

Moving Beyond Words was published in January 1994, also the year of her 60th birthday. This time, her friends threw another surprise birthday party for her and raised over $2 million in her honor for the Ms. Foundation. They had planned a $6 million fund, to be given with the express intent of allowing Gloria to disperse it herself. She was stunned. Bella Abzug announced, "She's Elizabeth Cady Stanton and Susan B. Anthony and Emma Goldman all rolled up into one—and she still doesn't gain any weight."[12] Age did not stop Gloria, either. The following June, she set off on safari in the Kalahari Desert in Botswana, Africa, and thoroughly relished the experience.

In 1997, Gloria saw the downsizing of Ms. magazine, which was once again running on a shoestring budget. Dale Lang was ready to sell his magazines to a print media-advertising salesman, Jay MacDonald, who was financed by Paxton Communications. Yet, as a media sales representative, with little experience in the publishing end of the business, MacDonald began to lose money on both *Working Woman* and *Working Mother* and pulled funds from Ms. to keep the other two magazines running. By 1998, Gloria was once again amassing patrons to take back her magazine. Ultimately, the consortium of feminist investors formed Liberty Media for Women. Although Ms. suspended publication for a while, it was back on the stands in March 1999, with the headline "WE'RE BACK! Wake up and Smell the Estrogen,"[13] and the publication continues to remain ad free. Of the new arrangement, Gloria said, "Thanks to the women investors who bought Ms. in 1999, we have not only been able to control our own financial destiny again, but to take time investigating proposals for the future."[14]

Yet, power modifications at Ms. continued into the year 2001, when Liberty Media for Women was assumed by the Feminist Majority Foundation, a feminist action and research organization with Eleanor Smeal, past president of NOW, as its president. Robin Morgan, who had assumed the editor in chief position at Ms. between 1990 and 1994, said of the merger, "The joining of Ms. and the Feminist Majority Foundation will ensure a successful and strengthened future for Ms. as the foremost communication tool for the feminist movement."[15]

SO NOT GLORIA

Before the sale, however, Gloria did something that made the world scratch its chin. She got married. The woman traditionally credited with the quotation, "A woman needs a man like a fish needs a bicycle," although she claims never to have said it, really believed in the premise.[16] She had balked at getting married all her life, and suddenly at 66 years old, she became the wife of David Bale, a South African businessman, who owned the first company to introduce skateboards in England. Gloria characterizes him as an intelligent adventurer and pilot who looks macho, but is somebody who "totally defies the idea that men are from Mars and women are from Venus."[17]

Gloria sees their union not as a husband-wife agreement, but as an equal man-woman agreement and said,

> Joining lives with David has brought a new companionship. It's great to have someone who knows all the disparate parts of my life; that's a first. Being married isn't better or worse than being single, it's equally happy but in a different way. If either one of us had been wanting or expecting to get married, it probably wouldn't have worked. I suspect you have to be able to say 'no' in order to say 'yes.' If we hadn't been content as we were—if this hadn't come as a surprise to us both—we couldn't have said 'yes.' And of course, if the women's movement hadn't spent 30 years equalizing marriage laws, I couldn't have done it legally; I would have been giving up most of my civil rights. As it is, I spent much of my life doing what women are not supposed to do. David spent much of his doing what men are not supposed to do—for example, raising his own children—so we came out in the same place.[18]

In 2003, Gloria Steinem seems a happy 69 year old, who still looks thin and elegant, belying her years. Her causes are still the same in some respects, as with women's rights and the pursuit of reproductive freedom, but she works toward the betterment of lives for women in Afghanistan and conducts self-esteem seminars around the country. She said, "And if we've begun to realize how deeply our self-esteem has been undermined by a woman-hating culture, the constant presence in our lives of a woman-loving group could help us free our authentic selves."[19]

Although some have touted the women's movement as dead, she sees it merely taking another structure. "Girls and young women are much more likely to be feminists today than ever before—as the public opinion polls show—but the same people may be even more so as they grow older and experience more that needs changing. Part of the problem is that the backlash has demonized feminism, and part is that older feminists don't always recognize the forms in which feminism now comes."[20] She sees the old feminist rap groups transformed as book clubs or networking groups and says, "Young feminists have singer/songwriters and events like Lilith Fair that we did not."[21]

As far as her health goes, Gloria still travels extensively and though she is definitely not ready for personal care, she probably needs a personal trainer.

> I often don't sleep enough, I never exercise enough, and I'm hooked on sugar, so I suspect most of how I look is due to genes. But because being overweight is such a family heritage, I do try to stay within ten or so pounds of my ideal feel-good weight. Any exercise consists mostly of walking in the city, running through airports, and sometimes doing yoga. I'm also a modified vegetarian. I eat seafood and dairy products but not red meat or chicken, as a result of having breast cancer.[22]

Gloria takes more of her time caring about others. For 34 years, she has made it her personal mission to change the world for the better, to make women equal to men in every way. She has given not only her time but also her money, freely and without reservation. Undoubtedly, her contribution to the world will long be remembered.

NOTES

1. The movie was released in 1985, with Kirstie Alley as Gloria.
2. Quoted in Heilbrun, *Education of a Woman*, p. 385.
3. Gloria Steinem, "Finally Real, the Feminist Recalls How the Fragments of Her Life Snapped Together to Make a Whole," as told to Francine Russo, *CNN.com*, 26 November 2001, http://www.cnn.com/ALLPOLITICS/time/2001/12/03/steinem.html.
4. Steinem, *Revolution from Within*, p. 263.
5. Ibid., p. 264.
6. Ibid., p. 266.
7. Ibid., p. 267.
8. Steinem, *Marilyn, Norma Jeane*, p. 8 (reprint ed.).
9. Quoted in Heilbrun, *Education of a Woman*, p. 377.
10. Five years after the book first hit the shelves, Gloria was still receiving letters.
11. Steinem, *Moving Beyond Words*, p. 122.
12. Quoted in Stern, *Gloria Steinem*, p. 439.

13. Quoted in Judith Shulevitz, "Wake Up and Smell the Estrogen!" *MSN Slate*, 30 March 1999, http://slate.msn.com/id/1002463/.

14. Quoted in "Ms. Magazine and Feminist Majority Foundation to Join Forces," *Ms.* magazine press release, 12 November 2001, http://www.msmagazine.com/press release111301.asp.

15. Ibid.

16. She attributes the quote to Noreena Dunn of Australia and says she does not want to steal Dunn's witticisms. She admits to having repeated the phrase, but she did not coin it.

17. Gloria Steinem, "From Ms. to Ms., Gloria Steinem Tells Barbara Walters About Married Life," interview by Barbara Walters, *ABCNEWS.com*, 18 April 2001, http://more.abcnews.go.com/sections/2020/2020/010418_steinem.html.

18. Steinem, interview, 2 February 2003.

19. Gloria Steinem, "Helping Ourselves to Revolution," *Ms.*, November 1992, p. 24.

20. Ibid.

21. Ibid.

22. Ibid.

SELECTED BIBLIOGRAPHY

PRIMARY WORKS

The Thousand Indias. Government of India, 1957.

The Beach Book. New York: Viking, 1963.

Outrageous Acts and Everyday Rebellions. New York: Holt, Rinehart and Winston, 1983; New York: Signet, 1986.

Marilyn: Norma Jeane. New York: Holt, Rinehart and Winston, 1986; New York: Signet, 1988.

Revolution from Within: A Book of Self-Esteem. New York: Little, Brown, 1992.

Moving Beyond Words. New York: Simon and Schuster, 1993.

Contributor to:

Cosmopolitan	*McCall's*
Esquire	*New York*
Family Circle	*The New York Times Magazine*
Glamour	*The Radical Humanist*
Harper's	*Redbook*
Ladies' Home Journal	*Show*
Life	*Vogue*
Look	*The Washington Post*
The Los Angeles Times	*Woman's Own*

SECONDARY WORKS
Documents

Chisholm, Shirley. Representative Chisholm of New York speaking before the House of Representatives on *Equal Rights for Women*. 91st Cong., 1st sess. 21 May 1969. *Special Collections Library, Duke University*. http://scriptorium.lib.duke.edu/wlm/equal/.

Joreen. "The Bitch Manifesto." *Special Collections Library, Duke University*. http://scriptorium.lib.duke.edu/wlm/bitch/.

Steinem, Gloria, Paul E. Sigmund Jr., and Leonard M. Bebchick. "Supplement to the First Edition: Notes on the Preparations for the Eighth Festival." New York, 1961. http://www.cia-on-campus.org/gifs/festival.gif.

Williams, Maxine, Frances Beal, and Linda La Rue. "Third World Women's Alliance. Black Women's Manifesto." New York: Third World Women's Alliance: n.d. *Special Collections Library, Duke University*. http://scriptorium.lib.duke.edu/wlm/blkmanif/.

Books

Anderson, Terry H. *The Movement and the Sixties*. Oxford: Oxford University Press, 1996.

Barghoorn, Frederick C. *The Soviet Cultural Offensive: The Role of Cultural Diplomacy in Soviet Foreign Policy*. Princeton, N.J.: Princeton University Press, 1960.

Barnet, Richard J. *Intervention and Revolution: The United States in the Third World*. New York: World Publishing Company, 1968.

Berry, Mary Frances. *Why Era Failed: Politics, Women's Rights, and the Amending Process of the Constitution*. Bloomington, Ind.: Indiana University Press, 1988.

Bloom, Alexander, and Wini Breines. *Takin' It to the Streets: A Sixties Reader*. New York: Oxford University Press, 1995.

Boyle, Peter G., ed. *The Churchill-Eisenhower Correspondence, 1953–1955*. Chapel Hill, N.C.: University of North Carolina Press, 1990.

Braden, Maria. *Women Politicians and the Media*. Lexington: University Press of Kentucky, 1996.

Brownmiller, Susan. *In Our Time, Memoir of a Revolution*. New York: Dial Press, 1999.

Cox, Oliver Cromwell, and Joseph S. Roucek. *Caste, Class, and Race: A Study in Social Dynamics*. Garden City, N.Y.: Doubleday, 1948.

Dow, Bonnie J. *Prime-Time Feminism: Television, Media Culture, and the Women's Movement since 1970*. Philadelphia: University of Pennsylvania Press, 1996.

Evans, M. Stanton. *Revolt on the Campus*. Chicago: H. Regnery, 1961.

Falk, Richard A., Gabriel Kolko, and Robert Jay Lifton, eds. *Crimes of War: A Legal, Political-Documentary, and Psychological Inquiry into the Responsibility of Leaders, Citizens, and Soldiers for Criminal Acts in Wars*. New York: Random House, 1971.

Gardner, Paul F. *Shared Hopes, Separate Fears: Fifty Years of U.S.-Indonesian Relations*. Boulder, Colo.: Westview Press, 1997.

Gilbert, Marc Jason, and William Head, eds. *The Tet Offensive*. Westport, Conn.: Praeger Publishers, 1996.

Hanlon, Gail. *Voicing Power: Conversations with Visionary Women*. Boulder, Colo.: Westview Press, 1997.

Humes, James C. *My Fellow Americans: Presidential Addresses That Shaped History*. New York: Praeger Publishers, 1992.

Isserman, Maurice, and Michael Kazin. *America Divided: The Civil War of the 1960s*. New York: Oxford US, 2000.

Jay, Karla. *Tales of the Lavender Menace: A Memoir of Liberation*. New York: Basic Books, 1999.

Jeffreys, Rhodri. *Changing Differences: Women and the Shaping of American Foreign Policy, 1917–1994*. New Brunswick, N.J.: Rutgers University Press, 1995.

Kolkey, Jonathan Martin. *The New Right, 1960–1968: With Epilogue, 1969–1980*. Washington, D.C.: University Press of America, 1983.

Levy, Peter B., ed. *America in the Sixties—Right, Left, and Center: A Documentary History*. Westport, Conn.: Praeger Publishers, 1998.

Lincoln, Evelyn N. "Young Man in a Hurry: John F. Kennedy as Senator, 1953–1960." Chap. 5 in *Becoming JFK: A Profile in Communication*. Westport, Conn.: Praeger Publishers, 2000.

Luza, Radomir. *History of the International Socialist Youth Movement*. Leiden, The Netherlands: Sijthoff, 1970.

Marchetti, Victor, and John D. Marks. *The CIA and the Cult of Intelligence*. New York: Dell, 1983.

Miller, Nathan. *Spying for America: The Hidden History of U.S. Intelligence*. New York: Paragon House, 1989.

Parmet, Herbert S. *Eisenhower and the American Crusades*. New York: Macmillan, 1972.

Polsgrove, Carol. *It Wasn't Pretty, Folks, but Didn't We Have Fun? Esquire in the Sixties*. New York: W. W. Norton & Co., 1995.

Quint, Howard H., and Milton Cantor, eds. *Men, Women, and Issues in American History*. Homewood, Ill.: Dorsey Press, 1975.

Rodnitzky, Jerry L. *Feminist Phoenix: The Rise and Fall of a Feminist Counterculture*. Westport, Conn.: Praeger Publishers, 1999.

Rositzke, Harry. *The CIA's Secret Operations: Espionage, Counterespionage, and Covert Action*. Boulder, Colo.: Westview Press, 1988.

Silvestri, Vito N. *Becoming JFK: A Profile in Communication*. Westport, Conn.: Praeger Publishers, 2000.

Simon, Rita J., and Gloria Danziger. *Women's Movements in America: Their Successes, Disappointments, and Aspirations*. New York: Praeger Publishers, 1991.

Sochen, June. *Movers and Shakers: American Women Thinkers and Activists, 1900–1970*. New York: Quadrangle, 1973.

Sosnick, Stephen H. *Hired Hands: Seasonal Farm Workers in the United States*. Santa Barbara, Calif.: McNally & Loftin, West, 1978.

Sternsher, Bernard. *Consensus, Conflict, and American Historians*. Vol. 9. Bloomington, Ind.: Indiana University Press, 1975.

Tobias, Sheila. *Faces of Feminism: An Activist's Reflections on the Women's Movement*. Boulder, Colo.: Westview Press, 1997.

Vestal, Theodore M. *International Education: Its History and Promise for Today*. Westport, Conn.: Praeger Publishers, 1994.

Wagner-Martin, Linda. *Telling Women's Lives: The New Biography*. New Brunswick, N.J.: Rutgers University Press, 1994.

Periodicals

Barker-Plummer, Bernadette. "News as a Political Resource: Media Strategies and Political Identity in the U.S. Women's Movement, 1966–1975." *Critical Studies in Mass Communication* 12 (September 1995): 306–24.

Breines, Wini. "Observation: Sixties Stories' Silences: White Feminism, Black Feminism, Black Power." *NWSA Journal* 8, no. 3 (1996): 101–21.

Farrell, Amy Erdman. "A Social Experiment in Publishing: Ms. Magazine, 1972–1989." *Human Relations* 47 (June 1994): 707.

Gibbs, Nancy, and Jeanne McDowell. "How to Revive a Revolution." *Time*, 9 March 1992, 56–57.

Gutner, Toddi. "A Feminist Icon Reflects on Money, Gloria Steinem Talks About the Financial Progress Women Have Made and Analyzes Her Own Strengths and Weaknesses in Managing Her Assets." *Business Week*, 17 September 2001, 116–18.

Hatch, Richard. "The 25 Most Intriguing People 2000: Gloria Steinem." *People Weekly*, 25 December 2000–1 January 2001, 68–69.

Myers-Parrelli, Anna. "Steps toward Transformation: A Conversation with Gloria Steinem." *Women & Therapy* 17 (1995): 477.

Schnuer, Jenna. "Steinem Makes a Bid for Ms." *Folio: The Magazine for Magazine Management,* 15 March 1996, 16.

Steinem, Gloria. "Advice to Old Fems." *Ms.,* February/March 2000, 93–95.

———. "'Women's Liberation' Aims to Free Men, Too." *Washington Post,* 7 June 1970, 192.

———, Joanne Edgar, Mary Thom, and Arthur Tarlow. "A Ms. Family Album." *Ms.,* July 1992, 44.

Thom, Mary. "The Making of Ms." *Ms.,* July/August 1997, 47–55.

Internet

Dreifus, Claudia. "Gloria Steinem Has Redefined Feminism, Publishing, Sexuality, and Now Aging. What's Next for the Matriarch of the Women's Movement?" *Modern Maturity AARP Webplace.* May–June 1999. http://www.aarp.org/mmaturity/may_jun99/interview.html.

Feminist Majority Foundation. "The Feminist Chronicles, 1953–1993." *Feminist. Org.* http://www.feminist.org/research/chronicles/chronicl.html.

Ms. Magazine Online. http://www.msmagazine.com/.

Redstockings. http://www.afn.org/~redstock/.

Smith College. "Agents of Social Change, Gloria Steinem." *Sophia Smith Collection.* http://www.smith.edu/libraries/libs/ssc/exhibit/steinem.html.

Theosophy.org. "The Study of Theosophy." *Theosophy Library Online.* http://theosophy.org/tlodocs/StudyOfTheosophy.htm.

INDEX

About the Author

PATRICIA CRONIN MARCELLO is a freelance writer who has written many biographies, including The Dalai Lama (Greenwood, 2003).